Advance praise for *In That Time*

"So many years after the Vietnam War, Dan Weiss has written an elegiac book about a soldier and poet who died when his helicopter went down in the jungle. A tribute to all soldiers who died in Vietnam, it's also a reminder that soldiers die at the will of people who may or may not understand what they are sending them to die for."

— FRANCES FITZGERALD, author of *Fire in the Lake*

"'Take one moment to embrace those gentle heroes you left behind. . . . ' America in the early seventies was too busy, too preoccupied, too contorted by the traumatic divisions of Vietnam to honor the invocation, a haunting line in a poem by a 24-year-old helicopter pilot, Major Michael O'Donnell. He died a few months later, in March 1970, shot down and killed flying a rescue mission. Now, a full fifty years later, Daniel Weiss is inspired to make up for unremembered time with a brilliantly reflective recreation of O'Donnell's Vietnam and the insistent questions in his sacrifice. Did we take what they left us and taught us with their dying?"

— HAROLD EVANS, author of *The American Century*

"They called it the pucker factor—the helplessness you felt riding in a chopper taking fire from below. It took half a century to dull those memories. Dan Weiss brought them back in one chapter."

— JAMES STERBA, Vietnam correspondent, *New York Times, 1969–1970*

"Dan Weiss has told a compelling story about the creative and artistic spirit of one soldier, but learning about Michael O'Donnell forces us to remember that there were more than 58,000 such stories of lives cut short; wives, parents, and siblings left behind; children unborn; songs not sung; and poems not written. Each of these deaths is like a jagged scar on the soul of our nation, made all the more infuriating for having occurred as part of a poorly explained and inconclusive war. *In That Time* reminds us what happens when leaders fail, that at the end of every bullet is someone's son or daughter, someone like Michael O'Donnell."

—WILLIAM S. COHEN, secretary of defense, 1997–2001

"*In That Time* rescues a young man's life from the jungle ravine where his helicopter crashed during the Vietnam War and was left undiscovered for decades. Like thousands of other soldiers whose lives had barely begun only to be squandered in that war, Michael O'Donnell had his hopes and dreams, family and friends. His poems about the war are still shared by veterans. Weiss examines O'Donnell's loss with meticulous and civic compassion."

—JOHN BALABAN, author of *Remembering Heaven's Face*

IN THAT TIME

IN THAT TIME

*Michael O'Donnell and the
Tragic Era of Vietnam*

Daniel H. Weiss

PUBLICAFFAIRS
New York

PublicAffairs
Hachette Book Group
1290 Avenue of the Americas, New York, NY 10104
www.publicaffairsbooks.com
@Public_Affairs

Printed in the United States of America

First Edition: November 2019

Published by PublicAffairs, an imprint of Perseus Books, LLC, a subsidiary of Hachette
Book Group, Inc. The PublicAffairs name and logo is a trademark of the Hachette Book
Group.

The Hachette Speakers Bureau provides a wide range of authors for speaking events. To
find out more, go to www.hachettespeakersbureau.com or call (866) 376-6591.

The publisher is not responsible for websites (or their content) that are not owned by the
publisher.

Print book interior design by Jeff Williams.

Library of Congress Control Number: 2019019037

ISBNs: 978-1-5417-7390-5 (hardcover), 978-1-5417-7389-9 (ebook)

LSC-C

10 9 8 7 6 5 4 3 2 1

For Sandra,
and for
Patsy, Marcus, and Jane

This book is not about heroes. . . . Nor is it about deeds, or lands, nor anything about glory, honour, might, majesty, dominion, or power, except War. Above all I am not concerned with Poetry. My subject is War, and the pity of War. The Poetry is in the pity. Yet these elegies are to this generation in no sense consolatory. They may be to the next. All a poet can do today is warn. That is why the true Poets must be truthful.

—WILFRED OWEN
1918, from a planned preface to his collected poems

CONTENTS

LETTERS FROM PLEIKU

If you are able
Save for them a place
Inside of you ...
And save one backward glance
When you are leaving
for the places they can
no longer go ...
Be not ashamed to say
you loved them,
though you may
or may not have always ...
Take what they have left
and what they have taught you
with their dying
and keep it with your own ...
And in that time
when men decide and feel safe
to call the war insane,
take one moment to embrace
those gentle heroes
you left behind ...

MICHAEL D. O'DONNELL
1 January 1970

A Note from
the Author

In the process of writing this book I have often been asked about my relationship to the subject of the Vietnam War and, more specifically, to Michael O'Donnell. After all, I was too young to serve and had no need to worry about the draft since the war ended when I was in my early teens. To be perfectly honest, like most people of my generation, the war in Vietnam cast a shadow over much of my childhood, and I was all too eager to see this enduring catastrophe fade from memory sooner rather than later. Moreover, I have spent most of my career in universities and museums as an art historian with expertise in the European Middle Ages and the classical world, not in twentieth-century American politics, military history, and popular culture. Finally, I never knew Michael O'Donnell. Why then have I decided to write about a young helicopter pilot I never knew, who was lost long ago, in a war few want to remember?

The answer is complicated, but I will say that I didn't really decide to write this book—I felt compelled to. I first encountered the outlines of O'Donnell's story and his most famous poem within the pages of Harold Evans's magisterial *The American Century*. I was deeply moved by the poem "Letters from Pleiku," which O'Donnell had written on New Year's Day in 1970. Unlike the Greek warrior Achilles, who eagerly sought eternal glory through sacrifice in battle, Michael O'Donnell was in that poem asking for something more modest and poignant: that we simply remember the people who sacrificed everything for a cause that meant so little. Even if the war should be consigned to oblivion, those who were left behind—on its battlefields, in its swamps and jungles, and even its VA hospitals—should not. In writing these words about Vietnam, O'Donnell was among the first to ask us to recognize that the controversy of the war was a thing apart from the human tragedy of the soldiers conscripted to enact it.

After reading the poem, I was drawn to learn more about its author and perhaps something of the circumstances in which it had been written. This did not begin as a book project, but rather as an act of curiosity, and a modest response to the poet's plea that we take a moment to remember. Yet, the more I learned about Michael O'Donnell, the more compelling his story became. It was a story about the life of a vibrant young man during a tragic time; a story that in its telling reveals much of what happened to America in the 1960s. The more I learned about his life, his war experiences, his personal sacrifice, and the legacy of his poems—not to mention his impact on the people he left behind—the more I began to understand the magnitude of his loss, and ours.

There is another, perhaps more timely reason that I have written this book. I wanted to understand how a democratic government, presumably with all the best intentions and led by people who considered themselves honorable, effectively decided to sacrifice the lives of its own citizens to advance an ill-considered and poorly developed political idea. If we understand the taking of life to be the ultimate human transgression, we need to understand how such decisions are made—in this case without a substantive understanding of purpose or consequences. Before the Vietnam War was over, the United States had sacrificed 58,220 of its citizens. The Vietnamese lost millions more.

By the time Michael O'Donnell was sent to Vietnam in October 1969, it was widely (if not publicly) acknowledged—by several US presidents both past and present and other government and military leaders, the soldiers doing the fighting, and the general public—that there would be no satisfactory outcome to the war. Yet, there was still no plan to prevent further casualties and death. Despite massive protests on college campuses and in city streets all across the country, the war would continue with thousands more casualties before the ignominious evacuation of the last Americans in Saigon from the rooftop of the US embassy in April 1975. One of those casualties would be Michael O'Donnell.

Within a few months of his arrival in Vietnam, Michael O'Donnell understood—as only a soldier can—that he was unlikely to survive, and that the sacrifice of his life would not alter the course of the war nor matter to his country. Through his poetry, written in the evenings after experiencing relentless days of trauma and death, all around and even within his helicopter, O'Donnell reflected on what was happening, even as he recognized that he was merely counting the days.

As I learned more about Michael O'Donnell and what happened to our country in the 1960s, I became committed to sharing his story. Perhaps it was because I grew up in the shadow of Vietnam and saw firsthand the destruction it wrought on individual lives and on the nation as a whole, that Michael O'Donnell's words struck so deeply in me. Although I was not particularly aware of the politics at the time, even as a middle school student, I was taken aback by what I perceived to be a dishonest government engaging in a pointless cause at the expense of real lives. The 1960s was a watershed era, with consequences that continue to resonate today. No longer do we assume that our government leaders are to be trusted, and no longer do we presume that they will do the right thing. To the contrary, we expect little from them and are usually not disappointed. Finally, largely through the devastating experience of the Vietnam War, the American people are far more skeptical about the concept of "American Exceptionalism," the idea that the United States is a unique force for good in the world.

I have carried Michael O'Donnell's story with me for many years. I have accumulated a great deal of material, including letters, poems, and even recordings of songs he made while at war. He was a very good singer and, in my view, a terrific songwriter. Over the years, I have also come to know many of the people closest to him during his brief life, including his sister Patsy McNevin, his closest friend Marcus Sullivan, his fiancée Jane Mathis, and many others. They have become good friends. I am grateful to them for sharing Michael and their own stories with me.

Michael O'Donnell died in battle 50 years ago, his unrecovered body left behind. His service to our country cost him everything; a sacrifice made all the more painful because he was sure it would be pointless. This book is first and foremost a story about loss and reconciliation, for an individual and our nation, but it is also a gesture of respect. For me and those who learn about his story, Michael O'Donnell was not left behind.

ARLINGTON

All quiet along the Potomac to-night,
Where the soldiers lie peacefully dreaming;
Their tents, in the rays of the clear autumn moon
Or the light of the watch-fire, are gleaming.
A tremulous sigh of the gentle night-wind
Through the forest-leaves softly in creeping,
While stars up above, with their glittering eyes,
Keep guard, for the army is sleeping.

—ETHEL LYNN BEERS, *1861*[1]

F or its reverential symbolism and pastoral beauty, the National Military Cemetery at Arlington has since the Civil
War occupied a central place in our national consciousness. Ma-
jestically situated on gentle hills sloping down to the Potomac,
its countless rows of uniform white tombstones today serve as a
poignant memorial to the ultimate cost of war and, equally, to the
importance of remembrance. Although ideally suited to such a
role, Arlington was not originally designed for such a purpose.

In 1778, the land, which was part of a vast plantation called "Abingdon," was purchased by John Parke Custis, the son of Martha Dandridge Custis and adopted stepson of General George Washington. John Custis, who had been raised on his parents' estate at Mount Vernon, was unable to realize any plans for his new property before he became a casualty of war, dying of typhus in Yorktown during the final months of the American Revolution. The property passed to his young son George Washington Parke Custis, who eventually renamed the site "Arlington" and developed plans for a magnificent estate along the Potomac that would rival that of his grandparents' farther to the south at Mount Vernon, where he also had been raised.[2] By 1802, "Wash" Custis began construction of a Greek revival mansion, which, when finally completed 14 years later, became one of the great homes of Virginia, offering both a commanding view of and easy access to the new capital arising from the marshland just across the river.

Arlington remained home to the Custis family for more than a half century. In 1831, when Custis's only daughter, Mary Anna Randolph, married her childhood friend, the young army officer Robert E. Lee, they too established themselves at the Arlington estate, where they eventually raised seven children, six of whom were born in the mansion. Yet, by the time of Wash Custis's death in 1857, the estate had fallen into serious disrepair. With Lee serving as chief executor and Mary inheriting a life interest in the property, the couple committed to restoring their home and improving the productivity of the plantation, supported by 63 slaves, who had been conveyed from the Custis estate along with the land and buildings.[3] Although Wash Custis had directed in his will that his slaves should be freed within five years of his death, Lee insisted that the slaves remain on the property until all debts had been paid and the property restored.[4] By all accounts Robert E. Lee was more demanding and less forgiving in his treatment of those under his care than had been his father-in-law.[5] In one account provided at the time by the *New-York Daily Tribune*, Lee was reported to have supervised the whipping of three escapees—including a woman stripped to the waist—and to have poured brine into their wounds.[6] Yet, Lee recalled the years spent with his family at Arlington as among the happiest of his life, "where my attachments are more strongly placed than at any other place in the world."[7]

With the Civil War on the horizon, the Lee family reverie was about to come to an end. Lee, as both an officer in the US Army and a citizen of Virginia, found himself in the untenable position of having to choose between loyalty to his country and loyalty to his state, which was preparing to secede from the Union to join the Confederacy. Although Francis Blair, on behalf of President Abraham Lincoln, offered him field command of the Union forces, Lee declined. Within a week of Blair's offer, he had resigned his army commission and had accepted instead command in the Confederate Army at the rank of major general.[8]

Lee's decision was a fateful one for himself, his family, and his beloved estate. Given their proximity to the Union capital, the family had no choice but to abandon their home quickly. Lee anticipated that the consequences would be dire: "It is sad to think of the devastation, if not the ruin it may bring upon a spot so endeared to us. But God's will be done. We must be resigned."[9]

The Union Army immediately recognized the strategic advantage of the mansion—untenably located at the nexus of North and South, Union and Confederacy—and appropriated the property, and within a week of Lee's decision had garrisoned troops on its grounds to defend the city. As the war progressed, the Union presence expanded in the area, and the lands adjacent to the Lee home were gradually put to use as a burial ground for the "indigent war dead," whose numbers continued to increase as the grim conflict continued.

The staggering losses of the Civil War created an urgent and unprecedented need for a military cemetery—and the Arlington estate was at the time both well located for such a purpose and otherwise available. But the Union leadership was also eager to confiscate Lee's property as retribution against someone they considered a traitor to his country. Montgomery Meigs, the Union Army quartermaster general and Lee's onetime friend, was especially keen to see Lee pay a significant price for his actions, and he wasn't alone. As the *Washington Morning Chronicle* editorialized at the time, a national military cemetery was

> the righteous use of the estate of the Rebel General Lee.... The grounds are undulating, handsomely adorned, and in every respect admirably fitted for the sacred purpose to which they have been dedicated. The people of the entire nation will one day, not very far distant, heartily thank the initiators of this movement.[10]

At Meigs's instigation, by war's end, Secretary of War Edwin Stanton had formally approved the appropriation of 200 acres of the Custis-Lee Estate to create a national military cemetery on land that had already been consecrated for the Union dead. For Meigs, it wasn't enough that the property be put into service as a military cemetery; he wanted to ensure that the Lees never returned, and for that reason insisted that graves be placed in the family garden located only a few steps from the mansion.[11]

The creation of a national military cemetery at Arlington was part of something larger and more enduring than simply solving the grim problem of what to do with these war dead; it was about more than retribution against Lee. Rather, as American historian Drew Faust has written:

> The war's work of killing complete, the claims of the dead endured. Many soldiers lay unburied, their bones littering battlefields across the South; still more had been hastily interred where they fell, far from family and home; hundreds of thousands remains unidentified, their losses unaccounted for. The end of combat offered an opportunity to attend to the dead in ways war had made impossible.[12]

A national movement focused on reconciliation, accountability, and respect for the dead had begun, the first phases of which were practical: to locate, identify, and bury those who had fallen in combat. As writer and former Union soldier James Russling argued at the time in an essay for *Harper's Monthly*:

> *Dulce et decorum est pro patria mori* is a good sentiment for soldiers to fight and die by. Let the American Government show,

first of all modern nations, that it knows how to reciprocate that sentiment by tenderly collecting, and nobly caring for, the remains of those who in our greatest war have fought and died to rescue and perpetuate the liberties of us all.[13]

Meigs, who ultimately saw beyond his animus toward Lee, had become a strong proponent of the government's responsibility to its fallen soldiers. He created a *Roll of Honor*, a centralized list to record the names and burial places for all identified Union war dead, and within several years was able to record 101,736 registered burials.[14] Although this number represented scarcely a third of the total number of Union casualties—the rest being missing or otherwise unaccounted for—it was a start, notably marking an important change in official policy toward the dead. The designation of Arlington as a national cemetery, among several others that had been created near former battlefields and hospitals, signaled a new recognition that our national responsibility was to honor in perpetuity those who had made the ultimate sacrifice for their country. As major general and later president James Garfield said at the Decoration Day ceremony in May 1868, "Here, where the grim edge of battle joined; here, where all the hope and fear and agony of their country centered; here, let them rest, asleep on their nation's heart, entombed in the nation's love."[15] The improvised graveyard at Arlington would become, within a few decades after the end of the Civil War, a national memorial.

Although the loss of their estate was all but inevitable in light of its new symbolic importance—as well as the practical problem that it was now the site of many thousands of graves—the

Custis-Lee family waged a long battle in the courts to reclaim the property. But it was simply too late; the growing cemetery was by this time well established, and it encompassed much of the estate, including the gardens adjoining the family home. Through persistence, Lee's children eventually reached a financial settlement to relinquish their claim, and never returned to live at Arlington.[16] Yet the Lee presence at Arlington had not ended. Within a few decades of the settlement, public interest in the leaders of the Confederacy, and especially Robert E. Lee, was on the rise in Virginia and other southern states. By government act, the mansion so beloved by the Lees became a public memorial and an official part of the cemetery they had so assiduously opposed. Thereafter, the Lee legacy and the national cemetery became uncomfortably joined in the larger story of Arlington, as they remain today.

With the passing of years, and the advent of new American wars, the US government continued the work of finding, repatriating, and honoring the remains of the war dead, particularly at Arlington National Cemetery. By the time of the Vietnam conflict a century later, Arlington had come to embody "the historical arc of the United States . . . where every hallowed acre narrates the growth of our republic and the affirmation of its ideals through sacrifice. Arlington is the History."[17]

PATRICIA MCNEVIN AND about 25 others—really just strangers who shared a tragic and excruciating burden—had on short notice been invited to gather at Arlington on the lawn of Section 60, a large expanse of mostly open space extending east toward the

Potomac. From there they could see in the distance, just above the trees planted so long ago by Lee and his surrogates, the limestone buildings of the nation's capital. It was August 16, 2001, and the morning unseasonably cool. The group had been called to this sacred place suddenly and unexpectedly—even if the funeral they had come to attend had been a long time coming. The service they were attending was one of more than two dozen on that day's schedule.

Although this was a peacetime burial, there was nothing routine about what was happening. This funeral would finally lay to rest seven soldiers of the 170th Assault Helicopter Company and Special Operations Group, who had died in Southeast Asia more than three decades before. The eldest in the group had not yet reached the age of 30 and the youngest was only a teenager when they were killed. The members of the Honor Guard who presided at the service were deeply moved to have the privilege of honoring their fallen comrades, even if most of them had not yet been born on March 24, 1970—several weeks before President Nixon publicly issued the command to extend America's military involvement in Vietnam across the border into Cambodia—when the helicopter carrying these men had been hit by a missile in the jungles of Ratanakiri Province. One of them, who was serving as an escort for the families in attendance, would later write, "While this was a war before my time, I still feel a deep sense of pride in their return. . . . I have the highest regard for my brothers who have fallen before me. I hope their return brings some closure and ease to the minds and hearts of those who care."[18]

For the families at the ceremony, closure had been a long time coming. Patricia ("Patsy") McNevin, now approaching 60, was there for her younger brother, a captain from Milwaukee, Wisconsin, named Michael O'Donnell. She was there alone, the only family Michael had left. Their father had died in 1987, and their mother, now in the advanced stages of Alzheimer's, could no longer remember either of her children.

O'Donnell, a helicopter pilot, had been in command of the lost aircraft and its crew. When it went down, he had been 24 years old. Many years later, long after the war had ended, Patsy learned that her brother's mission that day had been to fly his UH-1H "slick" across the border into Cambodia to rescue a reconnaissance team of American and Montagnard commandos, known by their radio ID as "RT Pennsylvania," which had been pinned down under heavy fire. In the face of grave danger, and without the benefit of additional air support, O'Donnell and his crew were able to reach the landing area and hold their position for four minutes—an eternity under battle conditions—while gathering the team of commandos. But on the ascent from the mountainous jungle valley, the helicopter was unable to escape the barrage of arms and missile fire emanating from an enemy burrowed into the hillsides. Just as air support arrived on the scene, O'Donnell's ship was seen exploding in flames before it disappeared beneath the jungle canopy.

Following the events of that day, the crew and passengers were listed as missing in action (MIA), although those who witnessed the scene were doubtful that anyone could have survived the fiery crash. But there was no way to be certain since, in the subsequent days and weeks, no attempt could be made to locate the downed helicopter and crew due to the heavy concentration of enemy fire in the area. Declared lost, the helicopter and crew were left behind, where they had remained for almost three decades.

Long after the wars in Vietnam and Cambodia were over, and few could remember the reasons why they had been fought, a Cambodian farmer brought news that wreckage had been found matching the tail number of O'Donnell's aircraft. After a significant recovery effort undertaken by a joint US and Cambodian team, the remains of O'Donnell and several of his crew were positively identified at the Veterans Remains Identification Station in Hawaii and prepared for proper burial. Once the forensic work had been completed, Patsy McNevin and the family members of the other soldiers were informed of plans for the funeral to be held only a few days later at Arlington. For the first time in 31 years, they would finally be able to say goodbye to loved ones and move on with their lives. As a member of the funeral party commented to Patsy, "Finally, no more letters, no more meetings." The years since Vietnam had been long and painful for each of them, just as they had been for the nation.

The funeral at Arlington, three days after he would have turned 56, finally laid to rest the young man killed so long ago in the jungles of Cambodia. He had posthumously been awarded the Distinguished Flying Cross, the Air Medal, the Bronze Star, and the Purple Heart for his actions on that day, and his commander had nominated him for the Congressional Medal of Honor. But those distinctions don't tell us who Michael O'Donnell was. The words that would be etched on his tombstone, just like the words on all the tombstones at Arlington, would reveal nothing about the person he had been, nothing about what moved and inspired him, nothing about his particular gifts, nothing about whom he loved and who loved him.

THIS BOOK TELLS the story of one talented and brave young man who became a soldier in a war and for a cause he couldn't understand, who didn't make it home. The Vietnam War claimed hundreds of thousands of lives, in addition to his. But if personal sacrifice is to have meaning, something of its cost must be understood, one life at a time. In his actions and his writing, Michael O'Donnell left a lasting legacy. In telling his story, we can learn something about a tragic hero of a forsaken war and how America lost its way in the 1960s.

This is not a book for scholars. The history of the Vietnam War and of its consequences for America has been written about widely. Nor is this a book primarily for those who lived through that era. Almost certainly, they remember what it was like. It is a book for those of us, and we are now the majority, for whom the war was essentially an abstraction; something we were too young to grasp at the time, or something that happened before we were born. But though it ended more than 45 years ago, the legacy of Vietnam is still with us; not only in our politics and culture, but in the losses endured by families and in the pain and trauma borne by veterans.

Just weeks after the remains of Michael O'Donnell and his crew were buried at Arlington, the tragic events of September 11 plunged the United States once again into a protracted and inconclusive war. The open lawns of Section 60 would soon be filled with new graves of young men and women who had sacrificed their lives to "rescue and perpetuate the liberties of us all."

PART ONE

For everything there is a season,
and a time for every matter under heaven:
a time to be born and a time to die;
a time to plant, and a time to pluck up what is planted;
a time to kill, and a time to heal;
a time to break down, and a time to build up;
a time to weep, and a time to laugh;
a time to mourn, and a time to dance;
a time to throw away stones, and a time to gather stones
    together;
a time to embrace, and a time to refrain from embracing;
a time to seek, and a time to lose
a time to keep, and a time to throw away;
a time to tear, and a time to sew;
a time to keep silence, and a time to speak;
a time to love, and a time to hate;
a time for war, and a time for peace.

—ECCLESIASTES 3:1–8

Chapter 1

AN ICE CREAM SEASON

Ideal voices and beloved
of those who have died, or of those
who are lost to us like the dead.

Sometimes, within our dreams, they speak;
sometimes the mind can hear them in our thoughts.

And with their sound for an instant return
sounds from the early poetry of our life—
like music in the night, faraway, that fades.

—C. P. CAVAFY, *"Voices,"* 1910[1]

In my ice cream season I've shared a lot of words and songs
and easy laughing...

—MICHAEL D. O'DONNELL, *1968*

To have come of age in the decade between the end of the Korean War and the assassination of President John F. Kennedy was to have experienced the most sustained wave of economic prosperity in America since the presidency of Calvin

Coolidge. Not that Michael O'Donnell or any of his classmates at Shorewood High School in Milwaukee were likely conscious of their economic good fortune, any more than they were of the real dangers being stirred up by the Cold War. Most Americans had been alerted to the potential for global war, and perhaps even nuclear Armageddon, by the Cuban Missile Crisis of 1962; but in the spring of 1963, when Michael graduated from high school, they were far less aware of the circumstances that had led by then to the gradual deployment of more than 16,000 American troops to Vietnam. And why would they be? Among the top 100 popular magazines published in the United States in 1960, there were collectively only 15 references to Vietnam, the majority of them brief citations in the weekly news magazines. Although the inexorable process of war making had already begun in the Eisenhower years, neither the press nor the American public was paying attention. The escalating conflict in Vietnam had not yet become a story of consequence. In the spring and summer of 1963, for Michael O'Donnell and his friends, the world was a welcoming place filled with promise and excitement.

Michael Davis O'Donnell was the quintessential postwar baby. He was born on August 13, 1945, just one week after the United States dropped the atomic bomb on Hiroshima and four days after it dropped another on Nagasaki, killing more than 220,000 people in all and prompting Japan's unconditional surrender and the end of the Second World War. In that same eventful month, the Communist revolutionary Ho Chi Minh and his nationalist militant supporters, known as the Vietminh, launched an insurrection against French rule in Indochina. But to Don and Bette O'Donnell, and to so many other American families in the years following the Second World War, the Communist rebellion in Southeast Asia was a distant and irrelevant matter. They were busy putting war behind them as fast as they could, and enjoying the postwar peace and prosperity.

The veterans of the war had returned to civilian life as heroes, celebrated by a nation grateful for their service and sacrifice. With the aid afforded to them through the GI Bill, many were able to return to school or begin families, and low-rate veterans' loans allowed them to purchase homes in newly emerging suburbs. There was, for the so-called greatest generation, a direct and tangible connection between their service to the nation and access to the American Dream.

Don O'Donnell, born and raised in Brooklyn, New York, studied psychology and labor relations at Ohio State, earning his room and board at the Catholic fraternity, where he was their champion boxer. There he met Bette Davis, a bright and attractive student from Grandview, Ohio. Shortly after they were married, they settled in Columbus, where their children were born: Patricia in 1943, followed by Michael in 1945. Although Don had been drafted in 1943, when Patsy was an infant, he had been unable to remain in the army due to chronic allergies.

The family moved several times in the next decade as Don pursued professional opportunities and advanced in his career as an industrial psychologist.

*Patsy and Mike O'Donnell,
around 1948.*
FAMILY PHOTO.

*Mike in elementary
school, at age 11, 1956.*
FAMILY PHOTO.

By the time Patsy and Mike were in their teens, the O'Donnells had settled in Shorewood, Wisconsin, an upscale suburban community offering almost everything a family, and especially teenage children, could desire. The O'Donnell home on East Kensington Boulevard was spacious and comfortable. The family had a beloved German shepherd with the unlikely name of Helsies Indiana William, known affectionately as "Bill," who, along with the kids, had the run of the neighborhood. Patsy would later recall the Shorewood years as happy ones for Mike and the family. Surrounded by supportive parents, many friends, and his beloved dog, Mike was an active teenager; he was popular with his peers, a member of Shorewood's cross-country and wrestling teams, and an avid reader. He was, however, then and later, an indifferent student.

Mike first encountered folk music in the corridors of Shorewood High, where, as a freshman, he met Bill Peckinpaugh, a classmate with a guitar, musical talent, and a keen interest in the folk music scene. With Peckinpaugh and others, O'Donnell began to explore a new world that became increasingly fascinating to him. He set out to learn the guitar, started writing songs and, with his new friends, formed a folk music group called "the Coachmen." For the first time in his young life, Mike had found something that completely absorbed him, that he loved, and that called on him to make a significant effort.

Later, Michael O'Donnell would title a collection of his poems and songs from this period, "An Ice Cream Season." The title was meant to reflect his feeling that this had been a carefree and joyous time in his life, but also one in which he was passionately committed to something difficult and personally meaningful. Although his interest in music was already keen in high school, it was during his years as a student at Whitewater State College, where he enrolled in the fall of 1963, when O'Donnell emerged as an accomplished songwriter and guitarist. From his first days in college, his primary interest would be outside of the classroom: in writing songs, playing his guitar, and participating in the vibrant folk music scene he found on campus.

Michael O'Donnell first met Marcus Sullivan on the Whitewater campus in the winter of 1963. Marcus, a talented musician and singer, was a sophomore who with his own folk group, called the Kingsmen, was performing folk standards by the Kingston Trio; Peter, Paul and Mary; Pete Seeger; and Odetta, among others. Marcus remembers vividly the first time he encountered Mike O'Donnell. "I was with the Kingsmen performing covers when I first heard Mike onstage at the Whitewater Student Union," he told me. "This was in December 1963. Mike had written a song about the very recent assassination of John F. Kennedy, called 'When You Think of Freedom,' which really knocked me out. The song was terrific, and it was written by a guy who understood before the rest of us that he had something to say." In short order Marcus Sullivan and Michael O'Donnell were performing together, and became close friends. "Mike was funny, talented, charismatic, and smart," Marcus said. "He was usually the center of attention, but he was generous and kind. He was good-natured, liked practical jokes, and he sometimes got into jams. He was always willing to lead the charge, but because he was so likable, he got out of most of them pretty easily."

Marcus Sullivan, born in Arkansas, had moved with his large family to Whitewater while he was in middle school. His father was an itinerant carpenter, and the family had to move often as he pursued prospects for work. But the move to Whitewater brought good luck, and the family was able to remain in one place long enough for Marcus not to have to change schools. His family was musical, and Marcus, also an accomplished track athlete, had been singing all his life. He had long been recognized as a talented vocalist, and singing became an important part of his life in high school and especially in college.

Soon after Sullivan and O'Donnell connected, they recognized that theirs would be an epic friendship. They shared a passion for folk music and, even better, they harmonized well and collaborated seamlessly. With O'Donnell writing the lyrics, the pair worked closely together to set out the music. Early on they performed their own songs, rounding out their sets with covers they admired, including Odetta's "It's a Mighty World" and a new song called "The Sounds of Silence" by two relative unknowns called Simon and Garfunkel. O'Donnell was particularly taken with the earlier folk version of the song that had been released on the album *Wednesday Morning, 3 A.M.* and saw great promise in this young duet from New York. Of course, like everyone else, Sullivan and O'Donnell were also influenced by Bob Dylan, Joan Baez, and the folk superstars Peter, Paul and Mary.

Like many of their generation, Sullivan and O'Donnell were interested in folk music because for them it was more authentic, socially conscious, and politically charged than rock and roll. The folk movement began to blossom on college campuses, first on

*Sullivan and O'Donnell
publicity photo, 1965.*
FAMILY PHOTO.

the two coasts, and then all across America. The genesis of the folk revival of the late fifties, and its mass-market appeal in the early sixties, can largely be traced back to 1948 and the formation of the Weavers, the first mainstream American folk group. Because of their socialist politics, the Weavers' popularity was curtailed by boycotts during the McCarthy-era Red Scare, but by the early 1960s, Pete Seeger, one of the founding members, enjoyed great success on college campuses nationwide, and his music captured the attention of the young musicians at Whitewater. During this period, Seeger played at San Francisco folk clubs such as the Cracked Pot and the Hungry Eye, and then went on to New York's Village Vanguard and the Blue Angel.

By the time Sullivan and O'Donnell began writing and performing, the children born in the postwar baby boom, nourished by the freedom and educational opportunities of America's postwar affluence, had grown into a newly empowered youth culture, increasingly targeted by media and marketers as a distinct demographic group. Rocked by the assassination of JFK, which occurred during O'Donnell's first semester at college, and inspired by the burgeoning civil rights movement, this new generation began to rebel against the values and priorities of their parents and commit themselves to change, both social and political. They embraced this new form of music, as well as rock and roll, and harnessed it to their vision of a better, fairer, less materialistic world. They brought guitars, banjos, and harmonicas onto college campuses all over America and began to play. The world was

Mike and Marcus
at Whitewater, 1965.
FAMILY PHOTO.

Sullivan and O'Donnell performing.
FAMILY PHOTO.

increasingly in motion, and young people were not only driving the change; they were also writing the soundtrack.

Sullivan and O'Donnell set out as a duet, writing their own songs and performing both at Whitewater and further afield, including in Old Town, a historic neighborhood and folk music enclave in Chicago. In clubs like the Fickle Pickle—run by Mike Bloomfield, who was to become a Hall of Fame guitarist for the Butterfield Blues Band—and Mother Blues, a particularly popular club run by Loraine Blue, a single mother and blues impresario who came to be known by all as "Mama Blue," they performed throughout the summer of 1965 with such well-known musicians as José Feliciano, Chad Mitchell, and Jo Mapes. Mapes, a seasoned performer with a national following, was one of several more accomplished musicians who gave them advice and support that summer. The duet first saw her perform at Poor Richards, a popular club in the heart of Old Town. As Sullivan tells it: "We loved Jo Mapes. She was there with her daughter, and they were both beautiful. She performed Gordon Lightfoot's classic 'I'm Not Sayin'' with a particularly intriguing guitar technique. After her performance, she taught us how to play it. She was terrific."

During this period, Sullivan and O'Donnell also joined a few friends from Whitewater to release an album under the name of *The Kingsmen Five*, which included several of O'Donnell's original songs. They both felt ready to embark on a serious career in music, and for O'Donnell, everything else, including academic work at Whitewater, was secondary. Although they were increasingly

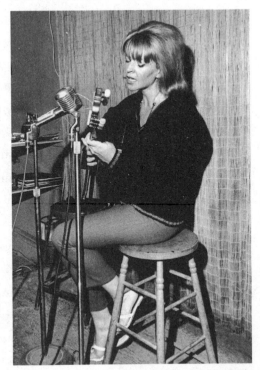

Folk singer
Jo Mapes performing.
GETTY IMAGES.

aware of the social issues roiling the country—especially the Cold War and civil rights—in the summer of 1965, US involvement in Vietnam was still only a small cloud in an otherwise blue sky.

THE YEARS FOLLOWING World War II had been prosperous and full of promise for American families, yet by the mid-1960s, the mood of the nation was changing. The civil rights struggle, which had inspired many, also brought to white middle America an awareness of the violent, hateful underside to the American Dream, as stories and scenes of brutality against African Americans aired nightly on national news and made headlines in print media. The greatest national security concern remained the threat of communism—more specifically its spread globally and the very real fear that the contagion would reach American shores.

In response, the Truman administration formulated a strategy of "containment," focused on preventing the spread of this perceived threat in key locations around the world, particularly in the Middle East, in the nations of Eastern Europe adjacent to the Soviet Union, and secondarily in Southeast Asia, where the communist Chinese were influential.[2] The goal was, at almost any cost, to shore up foreign governments—democratic or otherwise, as long as they were anti-communist—to prevent the Soviet Union from influencing or co-opting the governments of other nations. The American government sought to give these allied nations "the will and the ability to resist communism from within and without."[3] By 1950, with a new alignment between the Communist superpowers of the Soviet Union and China and the advent of an unexpected "major war" in Korea, the threat in Southeast Asia—known then as Indochina—became more urgent.[4] For the Truman administration, the rise of Ho Chi Minh's Communist regime in Vietnam was of special concern, and this led to a heightened commitment to the French-sponsored Republic of Vietnam, which it saw as a bulwark against Ho's expansion. Truman determined that American aid to the French effort be limited to materials and money, without any commitment of American troops.[5] Nevertheless, in January 1953 Truman passed on to his successor Dwight D. Eisenhower an extremely precarious situation in Vietnam. The United States had overextended itself financially by supporting the French, but believed it could not risk the collapse of Vietnam to the Communists if the French were to withdraw entirely.[6] The premise was widely accepted that the expansion of communism in one country would lead to further expansion, and ultimately destabilize the free world.

When he took office, Eisenhower intended to continue with Truman's strategy, fearing that any significant change might undermine progress, or perhaps more importantly, stability, in a critical region. The objective also remained the same: to prevent communist expansion in the hope that the Soviet Union would eventually collapse from within. Cold War strategists were confident that communism as an economic model was unsustainable and that time would be a powerful weapon. Eisenhower persisted with his economic containment plan for the duration of his presidency, creating new levels of dependency and therefore obligations that would persist for a long while thereafter. However, with the passing of time, the American investment became not only more costly but more essential. Political and military analysts came to believe that to withdraw American support would virtually guarantee control of all of Vietnam to Ho Chi Minh.

THEN IN 1954, the French suffered a catastrophic defeat to the Communists at Dien Bien Phu, and decided, after ruling for more than half a century, to withdraw from Vietnam. This was formalized with the signing of the Geneva Accords, which also divided the country at the 17th parallel into two separate nations. The North was ceded to the Vietminh Communists under Ho Chi Minh, and the South became the Republic of Vietnam under the leadership of Ngo Dinh Diem, a corrupt and widely criticized politician with strong ties to the American government. With this dramatic change in the political landscape, the balance of responsibility had shifted from the French squarely to the Americans, and there was no turning back.

A seasoned military strategist, Eisenhower understood the risks of unilateral intervention. He sought a more coordinated response from NATO that would draw other nations into the conflict. But when this was not forthcoming, the United States had no choice but to continue—and gradually increase—its financial support to the newly established republic and its controversial president.

The troubles in Indochina were real and growing, but they did not yet preoccupy the American government in the Eisenhower years. Though the investment of money and materials in South Vietnam was sizable, Eisenhower was able to buy relative peace and stability in this critical region and could turn his attention to domestic concerns, including civil rights and his prospects for reelection.[7] But while the immediate goal of containment in the region was met, the cost was growing and the entanglement deepening, forcing Eisenhower to leave his successor in a more precarious situation than the one he had inherited, just as Truman had done for him.

If the goal for John F. Kennedy in the winter of 1961was still to prevent the advance of Ho Chi Minh into South Vietnam and ultimately into the rest of Southeast Asia, there was no longer an option for American withdrawal. The Kennedy administration would be facing a complex and dependent entanglement with the government of the South, allowing for little possibility of success and no chance for a gracious exit. At the time of Kennedy's inauguration, there were about 900 American military advisers stationed in Vietnam—a legacy of both Truman and Eisenhower, who had sought a modest US presence to monitor the evolving situation. Before the American people had any real sense of what was happening, their government had already committed to a path with no good outcome.

Like his two immediate predecessors, Kennedy did not consider Vietnam to be a primary concern for his administration. In his preinaugural briefings, the new president had been told that Laos was the main source of trouble in Southeast Asia, since it bordered China, North Vietnam, and South Vietnam and therefore provided a route for communists to travel to noncommunist areas.[8] He did not immediately recognize the fragility of the situation that had been left to him in Vietnam, and assumed that the Diem regime "ought to be able to cope by taking no more than sensible advice and some material support from the United States."[9] Thus, he preferred a neutral option in Laos in the hope of preventing an all-out war that would necessitate the involvement of American combat troops in Southeast Asia, generally continuing Eisenhower's approach of taking "the minimum steps necessary to stabilize the situation in Vietnam."[10]

From the onset of his presidency, Kennedy was preoccupied with matters of foreign policy outside of Southeast Asia, and did not think it was feasible to engage in combat on multiple fronts. The most urgent issue for him was Cuba, a Soviet-supported communist outpost only a few miles off the coast of Florida, where just a few months into his presidency, he authorized an invasion intended to overthrow Fidel Castro's government at the Bay of Pigs.[11] The decision was Kennedy's greatest mistake, resulting in the defeat of the American-trained and -supported Cuban dissident troops by Castro's army within 72 hours. The Bay of Pigs fiasco was a critical and defining moment for the new president. The failure—which was public and spectacular—shook his confidence in himself, and even more in the CIA, which had masterminded the plan. It reinforced Kennedy's skepticism about using military force to address political problems, and heightened his distrust of his advisers not only in the CIA but also in the Pentagon, all of whom had too readily advocated the use of force before carefully evaluating alternative approaches or the downstream consequences of military escalation.[12] Kennedy regarded the Joint Chiefs of Staff as outmoded and unimaginative thinkers, all too content to resort to the approaches they knew best.[13]

This perception was further affirmed during the Cuban Missile Crisis of October 1962, when the president and his civilian advisers went toe to toe with Pentagon leaders, who vociferously advocated for the strongest possible military response to the newly discovered presence of nuclear weapons in Cuba. In this case, the Joint Chiefs recommended "a powerful air strike to destroy all military targets, a naval blockade to isolate Castro from all outside support, and an invasion to ensure the eradication of the missile threat and the removal of Castro from power;"[14] in short, a full-scale war against a crucial Soviet ally. In an attempt to intimidate the young president, General Curtis LeMay of the Joint Chiefs likened Kennedy's more diplomatic plan for a naval blockade with continued negotiation as "almost as bad as the appeasement [of Hitler] at Munich."[15]

In short order, much like his predecessors, Kennedy grew increasingly frustrated that his advisers could not offer a way forward in Vietnam that allowed for meaningful American involvement short of combat. He continued to reject any plans that called for the deployment of combat troops since he appreciated the risks involved, especially the possibility of another conflict like the Korean War. Rather than choose a definitive plan, especially one that he did not support, Kennedy opted to send additional advisers to Vietnam to collect information and help to formulate new approaches short of war. As a result of this plan, the number of US military advisers in South Vietnam grew from 900 to more than 16,000 during Kennedy's three years in office. This approach never met with approval from the Pentagon, which continued to advocate strenuously for a strong military presence to take the battle directly to Vietminh Communists under Ho's leadership.

Even during the most consequential moment of his presidency regarding Vietnam—the US-sanctioned coup and overthrow of Diem in October 1963—Kennedy managed to avoid direct responsibility. Preferring to have the South Vietnamese take action for themselves, the president stayed in the background, all the while reserving the right to intervene in the coup at any time. Writing to Henry Cabot Lodge, American ambassador to Vietnam, Kennedy instructed, "Until the very moment of the go signal for the operations by the generals, I must reserve a contingent right to change course and reverse previous instructions."[16] By avoiding direct involvement in the coup, Kennedy also limited his ability to control how the action in Saigon would unfold, including the unanticipated, grisly assassination of Diem and his brother.

Although Kennedy's strategy of minimal involvement in Vietnam was in some ways similar to that of Eisenhower, there was a major difference between the two: John F. Kennedy was foremost a politician, a first-term president with ambitions to be reelected and constantly preoccupied with public reaction to his decisions versus Eisenhower who was primarily a military strategist. Whatever Kennedy might ultimately have decided for Vietnam, he most likely would have waited until after his reelection in 1964 to implement it.[17] Of course, everything changed when the president was himself assassinated only three weeks after the murder of the Diem brothers in Saigon. Although it is impossible to know for certain what course of action he would have taken in Vietnam, in October 1963 he had endorsed the schedule proposed by Robert McNamara, his secretary of defense, and General Maxwell Taylor, his senior military adviser, to remove virtually all American soldiers from Vietnam by the end of 1965.[18] At the time of Kennedy's death in November 1963, American losses in Vietnam numbered 122—all military advisers who had been killed through their work supporting the South Vietnamese Army.

With the sudden transition in leadership from Kennedy to Lyndon B. Johnson, the American government's strategy in Vietnam was about to undergo a complete transformation. The new president, who had risen to power through a grievous public murder, was deeply committed to showing his strength and steadfast opposition to the enemies of the Cold War, even as his primary objective was a domestic one: to enact his vision for the Great Society.[19] Johnson had begun his long career in Congress during the Roosevelt era, and had witnessed firsthand the impact of the New Deal both on the nation and on Roosevelt's enduring renown. Throughout his term in office, his Great Society legislation remained the primary objective. Moreover, because he had come of age during the years of America's rise as a global superpower and remembered the extraordinary obstacles that had to be overcome, he was also determined to avoid the possibility of America's diminishment, or even worse, failure on the international stage.[20] As a result, he simply was not going to let the problems of a small country in Southeast Asia impede progress on his Great Society agenda, nor erode American supremacy in the free world.

Having assumed office under traumatic circumstances, Johnson was concerned to win trust internally and underscore the essential stability of US policy on the global stage. His earliest decisions on Vietnam were thus shaped by the policies of his predecessors Eisenhower and Kennedy.[21] Like Eisenhower, Johnson wanted to honor American commitments to the South Vietnamese in their fight against Ho Chi Minh and the Vietminh. As a new leader who knew little about issues in Vietnam and who was already intimidated by the intellectual heavyweights Kennedy had assembled to help him with foreign policy, Johnson was all too ready to accede to their advice, especially Secretary of State Dean Rusk, National Security Adviser McGeorge Bundy, and Secretary of Defense Robert McNamara.[22] These advisers, who had labored to find a winning policy under JFK, saw a new opportunity to move the new president closer to their own position, which was that the United States would have to escalate its involvement in Vietnam to make meaningful progress in advancing their containment objective.[23] They encouraged him to be more assertive, to more firmly take the reins, which he was immediately inclined to do.

The more deeply Johnson and his core team immersed themselves in planning for military escalation, the less patience they had for dissenting voices within the administration, in the halls of Congress, or elsewhere. They dismissed several advisers who advocated for a softer approach, and sought ways to reduce or avoid consultation with Congress.[24] Seeking action and consensus, the group's position hardened around enacting a military solution, and doing so sooner rather than later. If they could quickly dispatch the problem of communist expansion in Southeast Asia, the thinking went, the Johnson administration would be free to devote time and resources to such urgent domestic problems as civil rights, urban poverty, and health care. Many years later, McGeorge Bundy would observe, "Kennedy didn't want to be dumb. Johnson didn't want to be a coward."[25] On the question of Vietnam, both were playing defense.

Notwithstanding the emerging consensus that military force would be required to contain communism in Vietnam, the American government did not actually understand who its enemy was or why it was fighting. Ho Chi Minh, on the other hand, understood well that the key to his ultimate victory in unifying Vietnam was American ignorance. As he said in an interview with journalist Bernard Fall as early as June 1962: "The Americans are much stronger than the French, though they know us less well. It may perhaps take ten years to do it, but our heroic compatriots in the South will defeat them in the end. . . . I think Americans greatly underestimated the determination of the Vietnamese people. The Vietnamese people have always shown great determination when they were faced with a foreign invader."[26] The Johnson administration, by contrast, thought its partnership with South Vietnam centered around a deep commitment to independence from the North and the repudiation of communism.[27] The Americans consistently miscalculated the intentions of their enemy, "believing that Hanoi cared no more about South Vietnam than Washington did, expect[ing] that Hanoi would back down in the face of superior force."[28]

The pivotal moment in the escalation of America's involvement in Vietnam came in August 1964 in what came to be known as the Gulf of Tonkin incident. In the months following Johnson's ascendancy to the presidency, the administration had already begun working on a resolution for Congress to grant the president greater authority to take action in Vietnam without requiring congressional approval for each decision.[29] Johnson believed that he would need greater autonomy—and secrecy—to wage war in Southeast Asia, which would require the support of Congress, if he was also to maintain public interest and support for his domestic agenda.

The opportunity for the president to achieve greater independence from Congress arose when, on August 2, 1964, the USS *Maddox* reported that it had been attacked by North Vietnamese patrol boats in the Gulf of Tonkin. Two days later, a second attack was alleged to have taken place, which Johnson used as justification for retaliation, ordering the first US bombing raid of North Vietnam.[30] Immediately following these two attacks in the Gulf of Tonkin, the Johnson administration brought a resolution to Congress that provided authorization to "take whatever actions are necessary to defend Southeast Asia, including the use of armed force." In light of what appeared to be two unprovoked attacks on an American warship, the resolution was passed overwhelmingly in the Senate and unanimously in the House, effectively giving the Johnson administration a blank check to escalate the conflict secretly and without further approval of Congress.[31] It was at this point that the American presence in Vietnam became "Johnson's War."

The truth of what exactly happened in the Gulf of Tonkin in August 1964 remains a mystery, but it is clear that the incident was exploited by the new president and his advisers to secure congressional and public support for military escalation without the burden of congressional approval or public knowledge.[32] For Bundy, this deception was not criminal, but rather evidence of a failure of governance: "The Administration was almost forced to rely on the resolution and to make it carry a weight for which it was not designed." This, he said, "was not a crime of international deception but an error of democratic decision-making."[33] Whatever Johnson's motivation, for the remainder of his presidency the Gulf of Tonkin Resolution served as an excuse for secrecy and deception, and this is ultimately what led to his downfall, and was a major reason for the rise of public opposition to the war and to the federal government.

In misunderstanding the full range of issues that led the North Vietnamese to persist in the face of overwhelming casualties against a far more powerful enemy—effectively pitting Vietnamese willpower against American firepower—President Johnson set in motion a policy with unclear objectives and no discernable strategy for achieving them. Paradoxically, his fear of appearing weak would ultimately be his undoing.

DURING THE YEARS of Michael O'Donnell's "Ice Cream Season," culture and politics underwent rapid change throughout the nation and the world. Indeed, much of what defined American society when Michael O'Donnell arrived at Whitewater State was only a few years later largely incomprehensible to a great many in the post–World War II generation. For the young especially, Johnson's policies on Vietnam had placed the nation on the precipice of momentous change that would ultimately define the decade and what was to follow, both in America and around the world. By the spring of 1966, the war in Vietnam had become *the* national issue, with increasingly high levels of public concern about the purpose and cost of US involvement.

Not surprisingly, the specter of Vietnam had also intruded on Michael's Ice Cream Season. After the magical summer of 1965 in Old Town, O'Donnell had decided not to return to Whitewater. He was not keeping up academically and his focus was clearly elsewhere. To placate his parents, he enrolled at Centralia Junior College in Illinois, which was located near Springfield, where his parents had recently moved for his father's new job. O'Donnell hoped the academic expectations would be less rigorous there and that he would still be able to use an educational deferment to avoid the draft. But after several months of lackluster academic work, and an increasing sense that the war—and more immediately, the draft—would claim him as it had many of his friends, O'Donnell decided to take control of his situation.

Chapter 2

A SOLDIER IN THE SPRING

No great dependence is to be placed
on the eagerness of young soldiers for
action, for the prospect of fighting is
agreeable to those who are strangers
to it.

> —VEGETIUS, *fourth century AD*

and it was so easy
to be a soldier in that springtime ...

and in this springtime
I am a soldier again
and the battles are real ...

> —MICHAEL D. O'DONNELL,
> *"A Soldier in the Spring,"* 1969

As Michael explained to his parents and to Patsy, his decision to enlist in the army was not entirely impulsive. Although keenly interested in literature, poetry, and music, Michael was simply not ready for college. That much was clear. At Whitewater his grades had been poor, and at Centralia they were no better. His interest in music had carried him along and had been the source of his social life, but the future was less clear, especially since by leaving Whitewater, he had separated from Marcus, other friends, and the music scene that mattered so much to him. During his year languishing at junior college, Michael began thinking about his options. Like every young man at the time, he was worried about the draft, and, given his lack of a serious college record, he had good reason to feel vulnerable. All around him he could see that friends and acquaintances were being called. In 1966 alone, more than 380,000 men had been drafted, more than three times the number that had been called only two years earlier.

By the end of Johnson's first year in office, the United States had firmly committed to escalation in Vietnam, both through a sustained campaign of bombing, which was to continue uninterrupted until October 1968, and, beginning in March 1965, through the deployment of combat troops on the ground. At the time Michael decided to enlist, there were more than 300,000 American soldiers fighting in Vietnam, and given how many were being drafted, surely more were on their way overseas. If he were to be drafted, Michael knew he would have far less control over what might happen to him while in the army. As Patsy said later, "He enlisted because he knew they were going to get him."

Although it didn't make much sense to his parents, or for that matter to Patsy or Marcus, by enlisting Michael would have the opportunity to earn a commission as an officer and, if he qualified, go to flight school, where he could become a helicopter pilot. He had learned from Eric Renner, a high school friend from Shorewood, that there was a critical shortage of pilots to support the war effort in Vietnam. The amount of training involved to become commissioned as an army officer and then a helicopter pilot would take years, and surely the war would be over by then, or at least that was what Michael thought when he outlined his plans to Marcus. Moreover, aviation would give him a highly transferable skill, and he mused to Marcus that if their musical plans did not materialize, he could become a crop duster. He was 20 years old.

Michael's rationale offered little comfort to his family, all of whom were disconsolate about his decision. Patsy had recently left the University of Wisconsin–Madison when she had been accepted into the Peace Corps, and was preparing to leave, but at the request of her parents, she canceled her plans. The O'Donnells simply could not handle having both children away in distant and dangerous places. Bette was especially distraught at the prospect of her son going to fight in Vietnam. Patsy explained that her mother "felt that if she could take care of other boys, maybe God would take care of her boy," so in addition to working tirelessly in the hope of Mike's safe return, she also served as an active volunteer with the Red Cross, making "ditty bags" of donated socks, candy bars, and other sundries to be sent to the soldiers to support the war effort. Short of talking her son out of his decision to enlist, this was the best she could do. Michael's father characteristically said little, although he too was strongly opposed to his son's decision. Along with an increasing number of families, the O'Donnells now had a vital stake in what was happening in Vietnam. The war became quite literally a matter of life and death. Like so many others around the country, they were angry and distraught.

Only a few weeks after Michael enlisted, Marcus Sullivan was drafted, with orders to report for duty at Fort Leonard Wood in Missouri. If Michael had developed a plan to navigate around the war by pursuing an officer's commission and training as a helicopter pilot, Marcus accepted the reality that he would soon be on the ground in Vietnam as a member of the 168th Combat Engineers, scheduled for deployment in February 1967. He prepared to meet his obligation with the goal of returning home in one year, which was the required tour of duty for all draftees. During the Christmas holiday, Marcus married his longtime girlfriend, Charlotte Lee, and they took solace in making plans for their life together after Marcus returned from the war. Michael, then in the middle of his Officer Candidate School (OCS) training and unable to leave the base, missed his friends' wedding. He wrote to them a few weeks later:

> I must tell you Marcus how disappointed I was that I couldn't be at your wedding. . . . I want you to know that I wish you the very best of luck and that I am behind you a hundred percent. There are certain things that time and distance can't ever change and the way I feel about you two is one of these. Marcus, we've been through a lot of good and bad times together. . . . I guess we've done a lot of growing up together (I know I did) in just a few years. Our friendship I value as much as . . . well how ever much that kind of thing can be measured. So don't ever think you can't count on me, I'll be there old buddy.

*Marcus Sullivan in
Vietnam, 1967.*
FAMILY PHOTO.

Michael was slowly immersing himself in the culture and reg-
imens of army training, first to become an officer in the infantry,
and then when he qualified medically for flight school, as a candidate for helicopter pilot training. Writing to Marcus over the
winter, O'Donnell reported, "This OCS course is just unbeliev-
able.... You don't have one moment to yourself... everything
is planned; they say it gets better... all I can say is it has got to.
Christ, I don't know if I can take it. I have never been subjected to
such harassment in all my born days." Fortunately, Michael soon
got the hang of military training, writing to Marcus a few months
later, "The program here has settled down considerably. It's really
'no sweat' now that I'm in a routine. The weeks pass quickly."

Although his training was going well, the war itself was not. In addition to rising social and political resistance at home, the challenge of actually fighting in the jungles of Southeast Asia against a new kind of enemy was both formidable and largely outside the experience of the American military. The American army that landed in Vietnam in the early 1960s was more suited to fighting conventional land battles like those fought in the cities and countryside of Europe and on the islands of the Pacific during World War II, than to fighting in remote jungle terrain against an unseen and elusive enemy. If the purpose of the war was to contain communism from infecting and subsuming the fledgling democracy in South Vietnam, it was not entirely clear how such a goal could best be achieved.

An objective of the Geneva Peace Accords signed in 1954 was to provide time for the North, under the rule of Communist leader Ho Chi Minh, and the South, which remained loyal to the French, to prepare for a national election to reunify the country under a democratic government. However, the South Vietnamese government, confident that they would lose to the charismatic Ho Chi Minh, and with the support of the United States, refused to participate in the national election held in 1956 and to remain a separate nation under the leadership of the corrupt and extremely unpopular Ngo Dinh Diem. Following this breach of the Geneva Accords, the North decided on a course of war both to reunify the nation and to gain independence from outside rule. These goals were far more important to them than advancing the spread of communism, a crucial distinction that was lost on the Americans. Under the leadership of Ho and his capable general Vo Nguyen Giap, and with weapons and material provided by China and the Soviet Union, the North was both prepared for and committed to this war, just as it had been in the last one against the French. Moreover, it had learned from its experience that victory would require time, great sacrifice, and the accumulation of casualties. The South, on the other hand, was not unified behind its leadership, not fully committed to the American strategy of containment, and unprepared for war.

It was clear to US policy makers from the onset that the war would be fought in the South, below the 17th parallel. The risk of global escalation, including the active involvement of the Chinese or Soviets, was unacceptably high if the United States were to invade the North. This was to be a *limited war* against North Vietnamese "insurgents" and pro-unification Vietnamese living in the South, known as the Vietcong, who by 1965 held almost 60 percent of the South Vietnamese countryside. The challenge for the United States and the Army of the Republic of Vietnam (ARVN) was to defeat an enemy that was all around them, who knew the terrain and the culture intimately, and who was for the most part either literally invisible or indistinguishable from the local population. Under such challenging circumstances, it was difficult to know where or how to direct America's formidable arsenal. This was simply not a war that Johnson's advisers knew how to fight, even as they committed to a policy of escalation. As Marine Platoon Commander Philip Caputo wrote, "Without a front, flanks, or rear, we fought a formless war against a formless enemy who evaporated like the jungle mists, only to materialize in some unexpected place."[1]

Responsibility for developing a plan to escalate *and win* in Vietnam fell to William Westmoreland, a West Point graduate and distinguished veteran of both World War II and Korea.[2] A descendant of a long line of soldiers—his ancestors fought in the American Revolution and for the Confederate Army in the Civil War—Westmoreland seemed to be the perfect choice for this difficult command. He had graduated from West Point in 1936 as first captain, a position also held by Robert E. Lee, John J. Pershing, and Douglas MacArthur, and was known from early on as a proven leader and soldier's soldier. "Westy," as he came to be known at West Point, had risen quickly in the army, and became a major general at the age of 42, the youngest man ever to attain this rank. As plans for Vietnam began to take shape under the Johnson administration, Westmoreland was assigned to serve as deputy to General Paul Hawkins, Commander of US Military Assistance Command, Vietnam (MACV). Shortly thereafter, Westmoreland was promoted to four-star general and assigned to replace Hawkins. As American journalist and historian Stanley Karnow wrote of the new commander, "Westy was a corporation executive in uniform, a diligent, disciplined organization man who would obey orders. Like (Maxwell) Taylor, he saw the war as essentially an exercise in management—and together (Westmoreland and Johnson) . . . began to 'Americanize' the effort."[3]

Westmoreland's plan was to develop a counterinsurgency strategy that was predicated not on the acquisition of territory, as in conventional warfare, but on killing as many enemy troops as possible whenever and wherever they could be found: to wear them down in a war of attrition. The theory was that superior US

General William Westmoreland at a meeting in the Cabinet Room, October 1968.
LBJ LIBRARY PHOTO BY YOICHI OKAMOTO.

firepower could inflict heavy losses and, over time, such over-whelming force would wear down the enemy . Reported casualty rates of nearly 20 North Vietnamese and Vietcong killed for every American attests to the effectiveness of the strategy. Yet, as the war escalated and the body count grew larger and larger, the enemy did not lose heart and did not retreat. In short order, Westy found himself running on a catastrophic treadmill: the forces he destroyed were readily replaced by the enemy, which, in turn, required ever-increasing levels of American firepower and troops. At the same time the political climate in the United States was clearly shifting away from widespread support for the war to something resembling opposition, which had been building from numerous grassroots movements across the nation. In such an environment, Westmoreland had difficulty generating the support—and crucial resources—he needed to sustain the war effort and stabilize an ever-deteriorating situation.

BY THE WINTER of 1968, Michael O'Donnell had completed officer training and, as a newly commissioned second lieutenant, was ready to enter Primary Aviator School, located in Fort Wolters, Texas. He had decided to learn how to fly helicopters rather than fixed-wing aircraft. Aviation played such an important role in advancing Westmoreland's counterinsurgency strategy that the war in Vietnam would come to be called the "Air War." In order to kill North Vietnamese and Vietcong soldiers, they first had to be found, and this required consistent flows of reliable intelligence, much of it gained from the air or by small reconnaissance teams secretly inserted by helicopters into enemy territory. Once the enemy had been found, the United States required the capacity to move troops quickly over inhospitable and difficult terrain to engage enemy fighters. Throughout the war, helicopters played a critical role in providing this rapid troop mobility and combat support. The army established the first dedicated airmobile unit in Vietnam in 1965, and would be operating 4,000 helicopters throughout the region by the time Michael O'Donnell arrived in Vietnam in the fall of 1969. By the end of the war, helicopters had flown more than 36,000,000 sorties,[4] and would become the predominant image of the war in the media and for most Americans.

The 16-week introductory program at Fort Wolters was rigorous and intense. Washout rates averaged 30 to 40 percent in most

Mike and friend at helicopter school, 1968.
FAMILY PHOTO.

entering classes—which consisted of both commissioned officers like O'Donnell and enlisted men, known as warrant officers,
who were given a special opportunity to become pilots as a way
of meeting increasing demand. Students learned the basics of helicopter flying through a combination of classroom study and individual flight training with either military instructors or civilian
instructors, most of whom were former military pilots. The syl-
labus was rigid and comprehensive, both in the classroom and in
flight training, and each candidate's progress was evaluated every
day. Lack of acceptable progress generally resulted in a pink slip,
and three pink slips in a row meant dismissal from the program,

or in some cases, being sent back to begin the program again with a new class. Although most of the successful candidates found the experience to be interesting as well as challenging, they also found it to be extremely stressful. The intensity of the program was clearly intentional, designed to prepare new pilots with the emotional as well as the technical skills they would need to deal with the many challenges of wartime flying.

Learning to fly a helicopter was a formidable challenge, especially in conditions of war. In writing on the helicopter war in Vietnam, Philip Chinnery outlines the basics of flying a helicopter:

A helicopter is basically a flying disc, with a cabin suspended underneath. The helicopter will fly in the direction that the disc, comprising the rotor blades, is tilted. A smaller disc (rotor blade) is affixed to the end of the tail boom and is an essential part of the set-up. Without the tail rotor, the torque from the rotor blades would cause the helicopter to spin round in the other direction to the main disc, until it broke itself apart. Its function therefore, is to counteract the natural tendency of the cabin to spin around in the opposite direction to the main rotor blades.

To fly a helicopter, the pilot requires both hands and both feet and most of his fingers too. Strapped into his seat, he has a control lever between his legs called a cyclic stick, which tilts the whole rotor disc and moves the helicopter in the required direction: forwards, backwards, or sideways. In his left hand he has a collective pitch lever, which is pulled up and down to pivot the rotor blades, which increases or decreases their lift and is used to move the helicopter up and down. Both feet are used to operate two pedals on the floor, which control the tail rotor and are required to move the nose of the helicopter left or right. The rotor blades are connected to a transmission, which is driven by the engine, so a throttle is necessary to speed up the engine and thus the rotor blades. To do this, a twist grip is fixed to the end of the collective lever to increase or decrease the power as required. If this were not enough, various buttons are mounted on the handgrip at the top of the cyclic pitch lever, to operate microphone switches, trim buttons, hoist controls and, on gunships, triggers for the guns and rockets. The problem facing the fledgling helicopter pilot is that all the flight controls are connected.[5]

O'Donnell performed well during flight training, reporting to family and friends that he was learning a great deal and enjoying the experience. In a letter to Greg Stageberg, a friend from Whitewater State, Michael acknowledged the challenge: "I don't mind telling you that these helicopters are real bastards to fly, but I'm learning slowly and surely." He elaborated on his experience to Marcus: "Well, everything down here is going along smoothly. . . . I've got about 65 to 70 hours flying time now and I think the God Damned Army is trying to work me to death. We work very long days here . . . usually 10 or 12 hours of classes and flying. We have our weekends off, however, so I shouldn't complain." To take advantage of those weekends, Michael wrote to Marcus, he had bought a sports car, "an Austin Healey 3000 Mark III. It's a beautiful car, British racing green. I really can't afford it right now, but what the hell, you only live once. I haven't told my parents yet. You know how happy they will be about it." While at Wolters, Michael had rented a place in Mineral Wells, a small town a few miles away from the base. He also acquired a basset hound, whom he named Invader. Although it was in every way impractical for an unmarried army officer undergoing intensive flight training to have a dog, Michael was delighted to have the company, and to spend free time cruising around rural Texas in a British sports car with a basset hound in the passenger seat.

Michael also spent free time writing music, which he would record on tape and send to Marcus for comments and further edits. He also began in earnest to work on a small collection of

Mike and Invader, 1968.
FAMILY PHOTO.

Mike in Mineral Wells during his training to fly helicopters.
FAMILY PHOTO.

poems and songs that he was planning to write with Marcus and call *An Ice Cream Season.* In the summer of 1968, Michael wrote to Marcus of his progress with the volume:

> I believe that we have plenty to start with . . . if you like them we'll use them (the poems) or if you have some different ideas about the set-up let me know so we can work around a general concept. I get pretty excited about this deal, to be completely honest. It will be a lot of work, but I think we can do it . . . at any rate it gives me something to dream about and it's good to have dreams, right?

The themes he was writing about mostly concerned friendship, love, and romance—generally what one would expect from a young man in the prime of his life. Yet, there is nothing in this work about Vietnam, the army, or the war that was looming for him on the horizon. These were a thing apart in his consciousness, even as he faced daily reminders of what was ahead. For Michael O'Donnell, music and poetry were at that time a source of escape from the reality that was encroaching on him. As he wrote to Marcus, "There are a lot of things I could say now like how great it would be if I wasn't in the service and all the rest, but we both know we're getting too old for dreaming. So I'll make the best of what I got (which isn't so awful now) and we'll play it by ear."

One of the poems he had written was about his friend:

> If I were to open
> all of my world to you
> and talk of whom I loved best,
> even when we had to wander
> in our own times
> and even when miles and
> more months
> than a year were between us . . .
> I would tell you it was Marcus . . .

After completing his course at Wolters in June 1968, O'Donnell was sent to the US Army Aviation Center at Fort Rucker, a large training base in southeastern Alabama. At Rucker, he would learn to fly the Bell UH-1, commonly known as the Huey, which was to be the aircraft he would be flying in Vietnam. Although many variations of this model were produced during the war, their essential functions remained the same: to move troops and supplies, to engage the enemy in combat from the air, to support ground forces, and to provide medical evacuation support. The Huey was extraordinarily well suited to the war effort because it was durable and could be readily adapted to a wide range of purposes, among them defoliating the jungle with Agent Orange, evacuating critically wounded soldiers directly from the field of battle, and nimbly inserting reconnaissance teams deep in enemy territory. For these reasons, more than two-thirds of all helicopters employed in Vietnam were Hueys. Troop transport helicopters, which did not have rockets or externally mounted guns, came to be known as "slicks," owing to their distinctly different appearance from Huey gunships. O'Donnell had chosen to become a slick pilot. Through the training program at Rucker, O'Donnell and his fellow pilots were briefed on the special risks to pilot and crew of fighting guerilla insurgents in the dense jungles of Indochina. Yet, it is unlikely that any of them could be fully prepared for the experience that lay ahead.

As MICHAEL O'DONNELL and his fellow pilots mastered the skills they would need to survive as pilots in the jungles of Vietnam, many citizens of the country they served were challenging the whole idea of the war through an increasingly visible and powerful protest movement. In March of 1966, about the time Michael O'Donnell enlisted, coordinated protests against the war had been organized in New York, Washington, DC, Chicago, Philadelphia, Boston, and San Francisco. These were followed on

June 4 with a three-page advertisement in the *New York Times* featuring the signatures of 6,400 teachers and professors who opposed continued US involvement in the war. In addition to college students and teachers, public figures from across the political spectrum were joining the anti-war chorus.

Among the most important of these new dissenting voices was that of J. William Fulbright, chair of the Senate Foreign Relations Committee. Elected to the Senate in 1945, Fulbright was a powerful and highly respected leader of both the Senate and the Democratic Party, and had been a stalwart supporter of the strategy of containment in Southeast Asia during the Eisenhower and Kennedy administrations. Fulbright had been largely supportive of Johnson's agenda as well, even serving as Senate floor leader for the Gulf of Tonkin Resolution.[6] Fulbright knew Johnson very well from their years together in the Senate, and trusted that the president would be reluctant to use force, just as his predecessors had been. After all, throughout his presidential campaign, Johnson had pledged he would not commit American troops in Vietnam, saying on October 21, just two weeks before the election, "We are not about to send American boys 9 or 10,000 miles away from home to do what Asian boys ought to be doing for themselves." And, like other Democrats, Fulbright also wanted to do all that he could to ensure Johnson's victory over Barry Goldwater in the 1964 election.

Yet, Fulbright's opinion changed radically in 1965, as Johnson resorted increasingly and continually to the Gulf of Tonkin Resolution as his legal authority for escalating the war,[7] significantly eroding the Senate's role to advise and consent on matters

*President Lyndon B. Johnson and
Senator J. William Fulbright in the Oval Office, May 1968.*
LBJ LIBRARY PHOTO BY MIKE GEISSINGER.

of foreign policy. This was an issue of great concern to the long-time chair of the Senate Foreign Relations Committee. Having stewarded the resolution through the halls of Congress, Fulbright knew well that his colleagues in the Senate had not intended to give Johnson a blank check to escalate the conflict. At the same time, Fulbright was learning along with the rest of the nation more about the actual sequence of events that had transpired in the Gulf of Tonkin, which led many to conclude that the president had deceived the public about the facts as he sought greater authority and autonomy in escalating the conflict. For Fulbright, the president had violated the public trust and eroded the balance of power between branches of government, leading him to become an ardent opponent of the war, a position he was willing to take publicly.[8]

By 1966, Fulbright was calling for the president to seek a negotiated settlement, and to advance this position, began to hold open hearings of the Foreign Relations Committee to shed light on the facts and, for the first time, to encourage thoughtful and transparent debate on the war.[9] Consequently the Johnson administration was, for the first time, publicly exposed for its practice of deception, which in turn fostered meaningful support for the anti-war movement within the US government. Through his hearings, which continued for the duration of the war, Fulbright provided a forum for political dissent to be aired and debated, and for the government to be held accountable to the American people.

Others in the public eye also spoke out against the war in ways that galvanized the nation, including boxing champion Muhammad Ali, who upon receiving his draft notice, refused to be inducted, claiming simply, "I ain't got no quarrel with them Vietcong." Perhaps most important was venerable news anchor Walter Cronkite, who shared his skepticism with the public after visiting Vietnam in 1968: "To say that we are mired in a stalemate seems the only realistic, yet unsatisfactory conclusion."

Cronkite's comments came at a decisive time for the war effort and for the nation as a whole. With troop levels in Vietnam approaching 500,000, and with 30,000 Americans dead, public opposition to the war had become widespread and intense. The anti-war movement had given common cause to students, radicals, hippies, soldiers, veterans, priests, mothers, and many others,

Vietnam strategy meeting. Walt Rostow, McGeorge Bundy,
Secy. Nicholas Katzenbach, Secy. Dean Rusk, LBJ, Secy. Robert McNamara,
Amb. Llewellyn Thompson, Press Secy. George Christian, June 1967.
LBJ LIBRARY PHOTO BY KEVIN SMITH.

estimated at 6 million people who actively participated and 25 million more who supported the movement from the sidelines.[10] Unlike the civil rights movement, which was happening concurrently, the anti-war movement lacked a clear leadership structure since it consisted of such a diverse group of participants.[11] As a result, the Johnson administration tried to characterize the movement as marginal rather than representing the general opinion of the American people.

The beginnings of the movement can be traced to the fall of 1964, in the weeks following the Gulf of Tonkin Resolution, when a group of students and faculty at the University of

California–Berkeley organized a large protest on the university campus. The first widespread organized anti-war activity was the "teach-in" movement that began only a few weeks after the president had committed American soldiers to the conflict. In March 1965, the Universities Committee on the Problems of War and Peace declared Vietnam Day, during which 100 campuses across the nation held meetings for students, faculty, and community members to discuss the situation in Vietnam, focusing especially on learning more about the country and its 2,000-year history of fighting for independence.[12] These gatherings and events, which continued across the country throughout the rest of the year, had nourished the seeds of student discontent with the war and the direction of the nation, which would flower in the next few years into a national protest movement of unprecedented size, scale, and consequence. Even Ho Chi Minh understood the importance of the anti-war movement in eroding political support for Lyndon Johnson and his plan. He wrote in his 1965 report to his National Assembly:

> The American people have been duped by the propaganda of their government, which has extorted from them billions of dollars to throw into the crater of war. Thousands of American youths—their sons and brothers—have met a tragic death or have been pitifully wounded on the Vietnamese battlefields thousands of miles from the United States. At present, many mass organizations of individuals in the United States are demanding that their government at once stop this unjust war and withdraw US troops from South Vietnam. Our people are

resolved to drive away the US imperialists, our sworn enemy. But we always express our friendship with the progressive American people.[13]

By 1967, the war had become the "transcendent moral issue" for the nation.[14] Television news had begun routinely to expose the truth of what was happening by covering the war itself and contrasting what was being reported by the government with what was actually happening.[15] The erosion of credibility and the power of television combined to accelerate anti-war sentiment among the public, and ultimately increased support—or at least sympathy—for the anti-war demonstrators.

By 1968, in addition to grievous American losses on the ground, the controversial bombing of North Vietnam was result- ing in more than 1,000 civilian deaths per month, while having little discernible effect on the enemy. Media coverage of the ca- sualties and chaos belied the military's optimistic reports that the enemy was weakening. In January of 1968, Vietcong insurgents were able to penetrate the US embassy compound in Saigon; this was followed shortly thereafter by the so-called Tet Offensive, in which the North Vietnamese and Vietcong attacked virtually ev- ery American and South Vietnamese military installation within the space of several weeks. Although these military actions were not ultimately successful in achieving tactical objectives, they were highly effective in discrediting the reports of progress by the president and his military leaders.

As it became clear that public sentiment had turned against him, that he had no graceful way to admit to a failed war policy,

LBJ and Secretary of Defense Robert McNamara meeting on Vietnam, July 1965.
LBJ LIBRARY PHOTO BY YOICHI OKAMOTO.

and that his own party was prepared to challenge him for reelection, Lyndon Johnson's presidency became unsustainable. An extraordinary succession of events took place that spring of 1968. Johnson announced in March that he would not seek reelection for another term as president. In April the nation was rocked by the news that Martin Luther King had been murdered in Memphis, and then in June that Robert Kennedy had been killed in a Los Angeles hotel on the evening of his Democratic primary victory in California. Although it would not be reported for another year, the My Lai Massacre also took place in March of 1968. By the end of that year, polling for the first time showed that a majority of Americans were calling the war in Vietnam "a mistake."[16]

Westmoreland's war of attrition finally appeared to be working, but not for the Americans.

The presidential election of 1968 allowed anti-war activists to engage directly with electoral politics, especially after the shocking announcement that Johnson would not run again and the tragic, but galvanizing, murder of Robert Kennedy in June. When the Democratic Convention held in Chicago in August went on to nominate Vice President Hubert Humphrey despite his avoidance of the primaries, riots broke out, and the protestors refused to disperse, leading the Chicago Police Department to attack protestors and severely damaging the party's credibility.[17] Challenging a Democratic Party fragmented by its war policy, devastated by the assassination of its leading candidate, and then disgraced by its convention, Richard Nixon was able to win the presidency. By the summer of 1969, the anti-war movement, and more generally the radical counterculture, had become a fixture on the American landscape, as exemplified by the Woodstock Music Festival.

Throughout this turbulent and destructive time, Michael O'Donnell continued his training and preparations for deployment to Vietnam, which had been postponed several times over the past year. Although he certainly was following the dramatic events surrounding the anti-war movement, and more immediately, the progress of the war itself, O'Donnell continued to focus on his writing and, as always, the popular music scene. He wrote to Marcus Sullivan about his latest discoveries, "Have you heard Simon and Garfunkel's latest creation? That bastard Simon is fantastic. I've bought some real good albums lately, but there's one you've got to hear . . . it's called *James Taylor* and it's on Apple Records. I guess one of the Beatles had his fingers in the pie. It's just terrific. The guitar will drive you crazy . . . I recommend it highly." (Marcus, who had recently returned from Vietnam, received a call one evening from his old friend who insisted on playing the entire Taylor album over the phone.) Michael continued to be especially fond of Simon and Garfunkel, commenting on their music frequently in his letters and reporting to Marcus that the movie *The Graduate* was a "fantastic flick," which he had seen three times.

He had also made good progress with his own writing, which he described to Marcus: "I told you I was writing a lot so I have enclosed a couple of free-verse poems I've written lately . . . and right now I've got about twenty poems (of varying length) and ten songs." He reported further on his progress, "I've finally got somewhat organized and completed a beginning to an 'Ice Cream Season.' I've divided what I had into three sections."

In late winter of 1969, while training at Fort Rucker, Michael reconnected with Jane Hoge, a friend from Shorewood High School, and they became romantically involved. Jane had recently graduated from the University of Wisconsin and was enrolled in graduate school at Florida State University in Tallahassee, only a few hours from Michael's base in Alabama. During the spring and summer months of 1969, Jane and Michael spent a great deal of time together and fell deeply in love. It was a bittersweet time for them both. As was also the case in his interactions with Marcus and with his own family, Michael did not want to discuss the war with Jane. He avoided the topic assiduously, as Jane recalled later:

> Our time together was glorious and happy. Mostly what we did during the time we had together was laugh and love— sounds corny but it's true. Mike had an extraordinary and constant sense of humor and I love to laugh—we were a perfect match. There was much more time spent happy and being in the present than anything else.

Jane also reflected that "Mike was a little cavalier about the war. I asked him not to risk his life unnecessarily or to be a hero, and most frequently, I asked him to come back to me."

Mike and Jane at her home in Florida, 1969.
FAMILY PHOTO.

*Bette, Don,
Patsy, and Mike
O'Donnell, 1968.*
FAMILY PHOTO.

Near the end of the summer, Mike finally received orders that he would be sent to Vietnam on October 1, 1969. On his birthday, August 13, he began for the first time to write about what was to come:

> Twenty-four
> should be a great deal
> like twenty-three,
> waiting for the acne
> to find someplace else to go.
> Twenty-four
> will be a year
> lost to the war . . .
> Twenty-four
> will be the year
> I waited to be twenty-five.
> I shall be
> watching myself very closely.

As their weeks together dissolved into days, Michael and Jane quietly became engaged, planning to marry after he returned from the war. His future beyond the war—with Jane, with Marcus and the music they would write and perform—and the promise of better days, was now tangible to him. For the first time in a long while Michael could see where he was headed, and it made him happy. But first he had to get through what lay ahead in Vietnam.

On September 30, 1969, the night before he shipped out, he wrote to Jane:

Tomorrow I'll be leaving...
Tonight I spent some time walking,
I was going to think about
all the things I was going to miss,
but I tried not to think about you...

I wanted to put some important things
in glass jars
and tighten the lids
for the trip...
I would open them as I needed to,
Geritol for the soul.
I didn't want to think about you...

I kicked up the stones
along the alleyway behind the house
and tapped a stick I found
to no familiar rhyme...
I was not going to think about you...

You were all I thought about...

Chapter 3

Vietnam Winter

Autumn passed, winter came,
Winter wind and cold rain like a storm, friends,
And this lonely, empty landscape makes me sad,
Who can understand how I feel in the winter's cold rain.

I remember one day in Saigon,
I met a girl . . .
Perhaps she's married now
And I have nothing to wait for, friends.

I try to forget everything.
I cannot fight the life of truth,
So why be alone in the land of grief?

—DUC THANH.
"Remembering That Winter," written by a North Vietnamese
soldier in the bamboo forest, September 8, 1966[1]

The fall of 1969, the weeks in which Captain Michael O'Donnell completed his training and made final preparations to join the war in Vietnam, were momentous ones, both in Vietnam and at home. An ailing Ho Chi Minh died on September 3 and was succeeded by Le Duan, first secretary of the Communist Party in Hanoi. This was followed a few days later by the announcement in the United States that formal war crime charges were being made against Lieutenant William Calley for the premeditated and well-documented massacre of 109 Vietnamese civilians at My Lai. Later in September, President Richard Nixon ordered a troop reduction totaling 35,000 men as part of his ongoing Peace with Honor plan, an initiative designed to end American involvement in the war through "Vietnamization," meaning essentially the gradual replacement of all American troops with South Vietnamese soldiers. The plan also called for increased bombing of North Vietnam and, if required, the invasion of Cambodia and Laos as tactics to drive the enemy to the negotiating table. No one from the president on down thought that there was any reasonable prospect for a US victory; only that there was an outside possibility for a quiet and dignified ending to what had become a political and military debacle. As Henry Kissinger said at the time, "Johnson got us into the war quietly, now we are trying to get out of it quietly."[2]

Following the great success of the Woodstock rock concert in August—a celebration of music and global peace involving some 450,000 people—activists were planning a National Moratorium to End the War in Vietnam, to consist of teach-ins and demonstrations nationwide, for October 15, followed by a Moratorium March on Washington the following month, which would go on to become the largest anti-war protest in American history. Before beginning his long journey to Vietnam, Michael O'Donnell went north to Wisconsin with Jane to say goodbye to Marcus, Patsy, and his parents, and to leave his beloved dog Invader with his family. In a poem composed soon after he left home, he wrote about what he would bring along with him:

> This day was given
> to myself
> for the preparation of leaving...
> packing uniforms
> and one last looks,
> folding memories neatly inside of myself
> and folding underwear into bags...
> taking only what I need
> and hoping that it will be enough.
>
> *—2 Oct 69*

The final leg of his journey to the war was on Pan American Airways, a chartered commercial flight filled with soldiers destined for the war, which departed from San Francisco on October 1, 1969. During the journey, O'Donnell wrote:

> A day lost
> somewhere in the pacific...
> There are no days
> any of us
> can come back to,
> friday was a day
> I never had at all.
>
> *—3 Oct 69*

He arrived at Bien Hoa, a large military base and airfield about 20 miles east of Saigon late on a Friday evening and began the process of transitioning to his new assignment with the 170th Assault Helicopter Company based at Camp Holloway in Pleiku, a relatively large base located several hundred miles to the north in the Central Highlands.

During this period, he wrote several poems about the journey, his feelings about leaving Jane, and his observations about the strange environment in which he now found himself:

> Ben Hoa
> has only been
> a spot on a map until now . . .
> A place to come to
> when you finally have to come.
> Ben Hoa
> is more than 10,000 miles
> from a city in Wisconsin
> by the lake . . .
> They have nothing in common
> except one is where I wish
> to be
> and one is where I am.
>
> —*4 Oct 69*

During his journey to Pleiku, O'Donnell stopped at the American air base in the coastal city of Nha Trang, which dated back to the First Indochina War. Nha Trang was a tired seaside resort, replete with the bars, shabby hotels, and brothels that characterize such places in wartime.

I became a student
of Nha Trang today,
a city by the sea.
I approached it as a child
for I am still a virgin
of the war.
It's full of Catholic priests
and allied soldiers
and Buddhist priests
and other soldiers
and garbage
that seems to belong
exactly where it is ...
I can't say I learned a thing
and I couldn't find a whore,
though I'm sure there are more than a few ...
I couldn't find a need ...

—*7 Oct 69*

Once he had arrived in Vietnam, O'Donnell began to write more frequently. He soon developed a plan to record his experiences in poetry, and to gather them under the title *Letters from Pleiku*, in a manner reminiscent of the British soldier poets who chronicled their experiences of the First World War. By October 10 he had joined his unit in Pleiku, where, he hoped, settling into a routine would help to ease the transition to his new life:

I feel good that
at least now I have a place
to begin to settle down
and simply wait for the start

of a routine
and the rapid passing of time
and the days and the weeks
that it will all
spill into . . .

—*10 Oct 69*

Michael O'Donnell standing beside a Huey in Vietnam, 1969.
PHOTO PROVIDED BY JIM LAKE.

A few weeks later, he wrote to Marcus describing his situation, which, he was surprised to find, was not too bad:

It's been a month since I've arrived in country and several days later I was assigned to the 170th here in Pleiku. I can't remember whether you were ever stationed around Pleiku. It's really not too bad here, at least weather-wise, and things have been quiet with the bad guys also.

I've flown the last 23 days in a row, which explains why I haven't had a lot of time for writing. The days are long and I'm generally ready for bed by the time I get down in the evening. However, I finally got these two days off so I've been relaxing and catching up on my letter writing.

As I said, the living conditions aren't too bad here. I have my own room and the facilities here are fairly decent, to include an officer's club and flushing toilets, and sometimes even hot water. At any rate, it's more than I expected.

The days are long and at least the weeks go by quickly and this first month wasted no time with me . . . I've been writing off and on, small thoughts and poems and took some time to type several up for you. There's more and as I get them organized I will send them to you . . . I believe that I will call them "Letters from Pleiku," until something better comes along.

One of his poems written at this time captured the essence of his new life as a helicopter pilot in wartime:

October has
limped away
on David Fallin's
one good leg . . .

—*1 Nov 69*

THE 170TH ASSAULT Helicopter Company, known as "the Bikinis" for their exposure and vulnerability, was a light airmobile unit consisting of 28 Huey helicopters organized into three platoons, one with eight armed warships; and two flight lift platoons, known as "slicks," with ten helicopters each. Activated in 1965, the 170th had seen significant action in Vietnam and was among the most highly decorated aviation units of the war. O'Donnell, who now held the rank of captain—most of his fellow pilots in Vietnam were warrant officers—was, given command of the 10 helicopters in the second flight platoon, known as "Bikini Red," in addition to his active pilot duties. The 170th was one of several aviation units based at Camp Holloway; the camp's population at that time numbered more than 10,000 soldiers as well as support personnel and various Vietnamese camp followers.

The 170th saw considerable action while operating out of Holloway. Although relatively well protected, the camp remained vulnerable to frequent rocket and mortar attacks because it was situated in the northern reaches of South Vietnam, near significant numbers of enemy forces. During his first few months with his unit—and although he was platoon commander—O'Donnell followed the standard practice for all helicopter pilots in Vietnam by serving as the second in command, the so-called peter pilot, to more seasoned aviators. After gaining experience in the second seat and earning the vote of each experienced pilot in the unit, O'Donnell was given command of his own aircraft.

As had been the case at Wolters and at Rucker, Michael fit in quickly at Holloway. "Everybody liked Mike," said Jim Lake, a fellow pilot and close friend from his unit, many years later. "He was a talented performer on the guitar and special friend to a great many of his fellow soldiers." Jim recalled that Michael's music reminded him especially of the work of Paul Simon. He also recalled that everyone knew that Mike was a poet, and that he was chronicling his thoughts and feelings about the war and documenting their collective experiences. They believed that he was writing something important about what was happening to them in Vietnam, something people at home did not understand at all. As Lake said, "In the midst of a pretty grim experience in the middle of nowhere, where no one cared about us or what we were doing, Mike's poems meant a lot to us. He was telling our story."

Along with the other members of his unit, O'Donnell was flying combat missions almost every day, many of which involved transporting the dead and wounded from the front lines. His firsthand experience of the carnage and loss found its way into his poems, in both direct and indirect ways:

> Each of us
> is a can of tomato paste
> and though we may all
> not have the same label
> as we spin through the air
> when we land too hard

or get torn,
from the outside or within
we spill out
and stain the hands of everyone
who knew us . . .

—*25 Oct 69*

Somewhere in here
a kid named Davis died
with three other souls . . .
you could hardly say I knew him . . .
we passed in and out
of each other's days
without paying much attention . . .
Today he is dead on the side of a mountain
east of me
and all he's left me
is his void . . .
I found it sticking
to my ceiling
and the screens in the windows
of my room.

—*25 Nov 69*

In his letters to friends and family back home, Michael O'Donnell said little about the war itself, and he never reported on the details of his assignments. But his letters to Marcus reveal that it was becoming increasingly clear to him that the military situation in Vietnam was not likely to improve soon. In late November, he wrote the following:

There is no need to go into any detail about the war. Each time I begin to feel somehow apart from it all, I am reminded by the body bags I carry or the radio call on guard that someone is going down on a "May Day." Anyway, don't let anyone tell you that it's almost over, it's still as fucked up as ever, my friend.

The lives of helicopter pilots in the 170th, and elsewhere in Vietnam, were usually divided between days of stressful and dangerous flying and evenings back on base, where many gathered at the officers' club to drink and try to deal with the events of the day:

My rotor blades
beat against the air
and wear down the minutes of the day . . .
Pleiku evenings are too often
leaning against the bar,
each man must deal
with the war
his own way . . .
though the nights
are cool here
and find you underneath
a blanket in the dark,
the days are much too long
and warm
to be trapped inside yourself . . .

—*7 Nov 69*

After little more than a month in Vietnam, Michael began to fear that he was losing touch with his memories, which served as a critical lifeline to his past, and especially to Jane. By drawing on them so heavily each day, and not replacing them with new experiences worth remembering, he was feeling increasingly isolated and alone, as he wrote in a poem for Jane:

Like dreams
carved from bars
of Ivory Soap
you float by and melt away
with the passing of each day,
growing smaller
and smaller
until there is nothing
left of you
to touch . . .

—*10 Nov 69*

The daily grind of the war and the associated trauma that he confronted all around him—and within the close confines of his helicopter—were understandably wearing on him. Writing about the obvious injustice of the whole enterprise, O'Donnell asked the timeless question all soldiers eventually ask:

Heaven knows
I'm not so proud
of everything I've done.
I mean I've let some
people down.
And Heaven knows
there's so many things

left
I've got to do.
God knows I'm not so
sure of Him
these days.
He also knows why
people
are bleeding to death
in the back
of my helicopter
and He understands
how we can wash the
floor clean
and just one day later
forget He knows
anything at all.

—4 Dec 69

On New Year's Eve, Michael O'Donnell wrote the poem that
would become his best known, and he included it in a letter to
Marcus on the following day.

Dear Marcus,

I guess we are not very good correspondents. I have raced
thru the month of December and found I was not entirely
unhappy to see it leave. I am, right now, in the middle of being
positive I was never anywhere except Pleiku, Vietnam this
whole lifetime and am sorry to report that I've already played
the same good times over and over and they are beginning to

fade out. I think you must know what I mean. It's hard to make the old dreams last—especially when you have no one to make the new ones with.

At any rate I should not complain, it could be much worse, I could be a combat engineer or something . . . I have written a few things. I will send them later. I do want to give you this one I wrote last night:

> If you are able
> Save a place for them
> Inside of you . . .
> And save one backwards glance
> When you are leaving
> For the places they can
> No longer go . . .
> Be not ashamed to say
> You loved them,
> Though you may
> Or may not have always . . .
> Take what they have left
> And what they have taught you
> With their dying
> And keep it with your own . . .
> And in that time
> When men decide and feel safe
> To call the war insane,
> Take one moment to embrace
> Those gentle heroes
> You left behind . . .
>
> —1 Jan 70

I am convinced this will be the worst or the best year I have had. Ask me this time next year. Let me wish you a good year and when you have the time write me and take care of yourself.

> Until that time,
> Michael

In this extraordinarily moving poem, O'Donnell reflects on the theme of sacrifice, not for its ennobling capacity as is so often the case in war poetry, but for its rendering equal all soldiers, regardless of social position. For O'Donnell, death in Vietnam was not ennobling; his gentle heroes had not fought for a great cause; and the lack of a unifying national issue meant that their sacrifice was neither public nor glorious. In simple language, he asks that we honor these men by remembering them, and acknowledges that this may be difficult given the pointlessness of the war they were fighting.

IN LATE JANUARY the 170th received orders that the unit would be moved to Kontum Airfield, a remote outpost 60 miles farther to the north, deep within a stronghold of enemy territory and close to the borders of North Vietnam, Laos, and Cambodia. The base was small and isolated, offering little protection or access to the outside world. Indeed, during the period the 170th was there, the base was attacked by enemy fire almost every day, usually in the form of large but poorly aimed missiles. For reasons that were not obvious to anyone, the enemy followed a fixed and

Flight tower at the air base in Kontum, Vietnam, 1969.
PHOTO PROVIDED BY JIM LAKE.

predictable schedule in its attacks, with the missile fire beginning at dusk, shortly after the crews had returned from a day of flying. In turn, the pilots generally followed their own schedule, as Jim Lake explained: "We would return from our day of flying, grab a beer and then climb up the watchtower to observe the rockets." Because the missiles were crudely designed and launched from an improvised device, Lake characterized them as only moderately dangerous but very dramatic: "They looked like flying telephone poles and sounded like freight trains." In Kontum, the Bikinis had become as vulnerable on the ground as they were in the air.

Even the camp mascot was not safe:

a small brown dog
named herman
died beneath a firetruck ...
he left each sad man
who knew him well
a little sadder ...
not one of us
will ever become a fireman.

—*17 Jan 70*

The 170th had been sent to Kontum to relieve the 57th Assault Helicopter Company in providing air support for the most highly classified and dangerous operation in the war. A unit consisting of Special Forces soldiers drawn from all service branches, called euphemistically the "Studies and Observations Group" (SOG), had no official status as it was conducting covert counterinsurgency missions across the borders of North Vietnam, Laos, and Cambodia. Although the SOG was deployed throughout South Vietnam in many kinds of operations, its Command Control Central (CCC) was based in Kontum and focused on conducting secret reconnaissance missions into Laos and Cambodia.[3] Both of these nations had proclaimed their neutrality in the Vietnam conflict, but it was widely known that the North Vietnamese and Vietcong were staging operations, building garrisons, and housing troops across the border in Laos and Cambodia. Under orders signed by President Johnson in 1964, the SOG was charged with responsibility for waging a secret war in neutral territory. Their missions, and even their existence, was known to almost no one.

It was the responsibility of the Bikinis to support this effort by serving as air wing for all combat insertions and extractions "over the fence" into Laos and Cambodia. Each SOG reconnaissance team generally comprised three Americans and five to seven indigenous Montagnard commandos who had been recruited into the unit to serve both as soldiers and local experts in these exceptionally difficult jungle conditions. The soldiers assigned to the SOG, along with the helicopter crews supporting them, faced grave danger almost every day, resulting in high casualty rates. Numerous reconnaissance teams were stationed in Kontum, with several on assignment in the field at any given time. The Bikinis, providing the troop transport capability, teamed with gunship platoons such as the "Buccaneers," also from the 170th, or the "Pink Panthers" from the 361st Aerial Weapons Company, along with three fixed-wing aircraft, to provide on-site coordination for the reconnaissance teams as well as supplemental fire power. As a general rule, air support for each SOG mission required as many as eleven aircraft: four slicks, two to four gunships, and three fixed-wing aircraft. Such firepower from the air was essential since most of the insertions and extractions had to be made in live combat conditions.

Although the 170th was based in Kontum and SOG-CCC was located nearby, the missions were usually launched from a small, highly secret airfield in Dak To, which was even farther to the northwest and therefore even closer to the borders of

Cambodia, Laos, and North Vietnam. The compound at Dak To had a single runway, a wooden control tower, a canvas-roofed building, a storage bunker, and a small radio building from which the site commander could oversee the missions.[4] The pilots and their crews had no dedicated space at Dak To, and therefore were consigned to waiting out the long days between missions within the shade of their helicopters. After receiving their orders each morning in Kontum, the helicopter crews spent much of their time at the base in Dak To, enduring hours of relentless tedium in the stultifying heat, interrupted only by brief intervals of sheer terror.

During the weeks in Kontum and Dak To, O'Donnell wrote several poems expressing a growing sense of fatalism about his circumstances. He also said to Marcus in a letter from February 1970, "Christ I am tired Sully, I really am." Later that month, fellow pilot and friend Richard Davis was killed in a tragic incident resulting from friendly fire. Bill Watson, who had just arrived in Vietnam and was assigned to O'Donnell's platoon, remembered the incident years later:

> In my first days in the unit I got up early before everyone else (or so I thought) because I was new and worried about missing a takeoff time. It was still dark, about 5:00am. As I entered the latrine I saw Michael standing over a sink staring into the basin. At first I thought he was washing his face, but as I looked closer, I saw that he was just standing there crying. I didn't know if I should say anything and just stood there in silence.

Mike O'Donnell (left) with others in Vietnam, winter 1970.
FAMILY PHOTO.

When he saw me, he looked up and said, "It's okay, I just found out that we lost a crew last night. They were friends of mine." He then departed. I found out later that one of our gunship crews was shot down by friendly fire that night. Michael was close to one of the pilots named "Fast Ricky."

Deeply affected by this loss, O'Donnell wrote about it a few weeks later:

> I am breathing...
> Taking back everything and more...
> I have melted
> from the sheets into the net above me

and back into the sheets.
I have watched the ground
come to me
and I have crashed,
I have died
and I am alive ...
My God, where has
fast ricky gone?

—*26 Feb 70*

By early March, SOG reconnaissance teams were being deployed increasingly into Cambodia in preparation for an invasion—a crucial if cynical part of President Nixon's Peace with Honor plan—which was finally made public after the fact on April 30, 1970. But by this time, plans for many secret missions had been leaked—which resulted in significant levels of enemy contact during helicopter insertions and extractions, leading to high casualty rates—and the plans for Cambodia were likely no exception. Everyone knew that there was a serious security problem with the South Vietnamese officers assigned to the CCC, but apparently there wasn't anything to be done about it. (After the war it was discovered that a high-ranking South Vietnamese officer with access to the SOG mission plans was actually a North Vietnamese agent who had been feeding this secret information to the enemy.)

In anticipation of the impending invasion, on March 21, Reconnaissance Team (RT) Pennsylvania was deployed in the

Jim Lake in Vietnam, at age 18, 1969.
PHOTO PROVIDED BY JIM LAKE.

"Dragon's Tail," a mountainous region in Ratanakiri Province, Cambodia, about 14 miles beyond the border. Their five-day mission was to gain intelligence on the size and movements of enemy forces. The team on the ground consisted of three Americans: Lieutenant Jerry Pool, who led the mission; Sergeant First Class John Boronski; and Staff Sergeant Gary Harned. They were joined by five Montagnard commandos. Jim Lake and his crew inserted the team by helicopter early on Saturday morning. But since the location of the landing zone had been leaked, the team came into contact with the enemy shortly after the men were on the ground. Under the circumstances this was a normal occurrence; the team was not unduly concerned at having had enemy contact so quickly, nor in the early hours were they yet distracted from their mission objective.

In the midst of his SOG work at Dak To, and just a few days before RT Pennsylvania had been inserted, Michael had written:

I have tasted the air
in the early morning, before the sun
and before the day . . .
I have let it run all
down my face
and stain my clothes
and I have learned to wash myself
with the part of the day
that remains . . .
I am dying in the sun at Dak To . . .
I am each day
becoming less interested
in the way the morning tastes,
and I am dying in the sun at Dak To . . .
and I am dying in the sun at Dak To . . .

—*18 March 70*

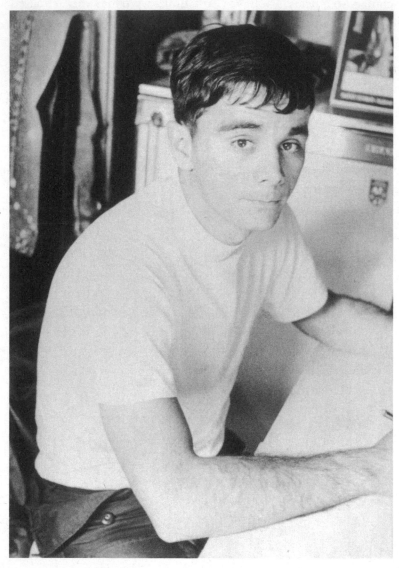

Mike at his writing desk in Vietnam, winter 1970.

Chapter 4

THE MISSION

The fires are grey; no star, no sign
Winks from the breathing darkness of the carrier
Where the pilot circles for his wingman; where,
Gliding above the cities' shells, a stubborn eye
Among the embers of the nations, achingly
Tracing the circles of that worn, unchanging no—
The lives' long war—the pilot sleeps.

—RANDALL JARRELL, *"The Dead Wingman"*[1]

O n the morning of March 24, 1970, as the pilots gathered on the flight line in Kontum, they were informed that RT Pennsylvania was in serious trouble three days into its mission. On this Tuesday morning, O'Donnell's platoon was ordered to the mission staging area in Dak To, where they were to prepare for an emergency rescue extraction, and provide routine support for the other groups that were currently in the field or ready to be deployed.[2]

O'Donnell and the others were told that, three days after their insertion into enemy territory, Lieutenant Jerry Pool and the others were still on the run, exchanging fire with the North Vietnamese counter-reconnaissance teams who were in close pursuit. Moving farther into the mountains, they were forced to cut through the dense jungle at an exhausting pace, confronting not only the enemy but also poisonous snakes and dangerous terrain. To make matters worse, each time they paused, the enemy pressed in, making contact and forcing the team to resume the chase farther into the mountains to avoid capture. The first night they were able to get some much-needed rest, but by morning they were on the run again with the enemy in close pursuit. By nightfall of the second night, Pool and his team had established a constant dodge-and-ambush routine, fighting against a large and formidable force of enemy troops. Nothing they tried was working. Unable to shake their adversaries and now unable to rest, the team was nearing exhaustion, and their supply of ammunition was diminishing quickly. Soon thereafter, the North Vietnamese added tracking dogs to the chase. It was clear to Pool that the mission was lost and that the team was facing a crisis.

By the morning of the third day, March 24, the team could see that they were continuing to lose ground to the North Vietnamese trackers, which meant that capture or worse was increasingly likely. With his options running out, Pool declared a tactical emergency, calling on his radio for an immediate "prairie fire extraction," which meant that the Bikinis would need to rescue the commando team in the face of substantial enemy fire. Pool reported to SOG Command that his team had gone as far as it could, that the mission had been compromised, and, most important, that time was running out if they were to avoid capture or death. After relaying their emergency situation to SOG Command at Dak To, the team continued to run, resuming their evasive tactics up the side of the next mountain. If help did not arrive soon, the team was sure to be overrun.

Four slicks from Bikini Red and four Cobra gunships from the 361st Aerial Weapons Company's Pink Panthers platoon were briefed on the situation and prepared to make the extraction, which was going to be exceptionally dangerous given the number of enemy forces on the ground and the unfavorable conditions for a helicopter landing. O'Donnell's friend, Jim Lake, was to be in command on this mission. Lake would be flying with his co-pilot Jonny Kemper, who was himself a veteran pilot and former Green Beret. Lake had been in Vietnam for more than 11 months, making him the senior pilot in the unit. Kemper, too, had been in country for many months but, for much of his tour, he had flown a gunship with the Buccaneers. Although relatively new to slicks, Kemper was a steady and capable pilot.

O'Donnell, the Red Platoon leader, flew under the command of Lake on this mission. While senior in rank, he was junior in experience, so he flew wing rather than lead. On SOG missions, experience meant better odds for survival for the crews and the teams. By mutual agreement, the most experienced aircraft commander led the mission, regardless of rank. O'Donnell's copilot was Warrant Officer John Hoskin, who had been in Vietnam for only a few weeks. His crew consisted of chief Rudy Becerra and door gunner Berman Ganoe, both experienced veterans of many SOG missions.

By midmorning the Bikinis and Panthers were in Dak To, fully prepared and waiting in the hot sun for orders from SOG Command, which was in constant radio communication with Pool and his team. As soon as RT Pennsylvania came within range of a feasible landing zone, the Huey helicopters would be called upon to pull them out with the support of the Panther gunships. The flight into Cambodia would take about 20 minutes.

Meanwhile, an air force observation airplane containing the forward airborne controller (FAC), also known on SOG missions as the "Covey Rider," was circling slowly in the sky high above, to oversee the mission and coordinate the action below. The Covey Rider, maintaining constant radio contact with Pool and Sergeant First Class John Boronski, was having difficulty finding a feasible landing zone within close range of the team in the mountainous terrain. Pool reported that his team continued to run and ambush all morning, but their pursuers were right behind them. Master Sergeant Charles Septer, who was serving as Covey Rider, knew that he had very little time to get help to the team if they were going to make it. As an interim measure, he called for additional fixed-wing air support in the form of two A1-H Skyraiders, known as "Spads." These propeller-driven fighter planes, which were first used during the Korean War, proved especially useful in supporting the SOG missions because they flew slowly enough to provide excellent close-in air support to the teams on the ground, and could remain in the air for extended periods of time.

Initially, the arrival of the Spads provided welcome relief to RT Pennsylvania, allowing them to gain some distance from the advancing enemy as the planes dropped cluster bombs and napalm around the team's perimeter. Although the napalm succeeded in slowing down the enemy, it also started numerous fires. March was dry season in Cambodia, and the dense growth of the jungle was especially susceptible to fire. Pool soon radioed Covey Rider Septer to say the advancing fires had become as much of a threat as the advancing enemy. As the Spads continued to attack the surrounding area, Septer was finalizing an extraction plan. He radioed back to Pool, directing the team to move southwest, toward the bottom of a steep valley with high canyon walls that was located nearby. Pool acknowledged the transmission and repeated that the North Vietnamese army was closing in, and that he did not think the team could make it to that location without additional air coverage. At about 1:00 p.m., the Covey Rider called in the Panther helicopter gunships to provide close air support as RT Pennsylvania made its way to the landing zone.

The Panthers scrambled, accompanied by Lake and O'Donnell as backup support for the gunships. After an approximately 20-minute flight, the four gunships and two slicks were in position to make the emergency extraction. They were joined by the Spads, which continued to circle slowly in the sky above. The Covey Rider directed the helicopters to Pennsylvania's location, and then, based on reports from Pool, gave them the coordinates for the enemy positions. Two Cobra teams engaged immediately, firing their rockets at the enemy positions around Pennsylvania. The remaining Cobra teams and the two slicks orbited above the action at 1,500 feet, waiting for the team to reach the landing zone. After they expended their rockets and ammunition, the two Cobras withdrew from the area, returning to Dak To for fuel and ammunition.

On the ground, the situation facing RT Pennsylvania continued to deteriorate. Pool reported that they had resumed contact with the enemy, which was again slowing their progress. To reach the landing zone from their position, they would have to descend to the valley floor, and then move southwest a considerable distance. It was clear to all that the situation had now become desperate for the eight exhausted men on the ground.

In the sky above, Lake noted that the Hueys had little more than one hour of fuel remaining. Considering the team's slow progress, he estimated that the slicks would need to refuel before Pennsylvania could reach the landing zone. Lake therefore instructed O'Donnell to remain on station as long as possible to cover the Cobras while the gunships continued their attack. In the meantime, Lake would return to Dak To, refuel and collect the other two slicks so that he could make the extraction of RT Pennsylvania upon his return.

Racing back to Dak To, Lake and Kemper discussed the best way to perform what was sure to be an exceptionally difficult extraction. As they were refueling, Lake briefed the other two slicks on the current situation. Not only was RT Pennsylvania in desperate need of rescue but O'Donnell and the gunships were quickly running out of fuel. Time was critical. As Lake and his team made their way back into Cambodia, the pilots continued to monitor the calls between the Covey Rider and Pool.

The intervening minutes had been harrowing ones for Pool and RT Pennsylvania. In continuous contact with the enemy, they were now racing headlong through the dense jungle toward the landing zone. Meanwhile, Lake and the other slicks were flying at full speed back into Cambodia—they were approximately 10 minutes away. As the commandos stumbled down the steep slope toward the rescue point, Pool fell and badly injured his ankle. He reported that the enemy was right behind them, the fires were closing in, and he could not move any farther. He asked Covey Rider Septer where the extraction team was, Septer replied that they were on their way. Pool then looked up to the sky and saw O'Donnell orbiting in the distance. He desperately called out to him for immediate help.

Like all helicopter pilots in Vietnam, Michael O'Donnell was committed foremost to rescuing fellow soldiers who were injured or in danger. Without hesitation, O'Donnell told Septer that he would make the extraction alone. Lake intercepted the transmission, telling O'Donnell that they were only minutes away and to wait for reinforcements. However, it was clear to O'Donnell that Pool and the others didn't have a few minutes. This was the end of the line for them. So he was going in now on his own. Followed by the team of Cobras, O'Donnell dropped quickly from his holding position in the sky. Racing down between the canyon walls deep into the valley and through a small opening in the jungle canopy, he slowed to a hover just above the landing zone. Completely exposed, O'Donnell and his team then held their position while the reconnaissance team raced through the dense undergrowth toward the aircraft. As the minutes ticked by, Lake and the other slicks arrived overhead. After about four minutes, an eternity under such conditions, O'Donnell started to move away from the landing zone, maneuvering his helicopter carefully up through the narrow opening in the trees. Slowly gathering speed, he began to climb toward the sky. At about 200 feet above the ground he reported, "I've got all eight, I'm coming out," and he began to accelerate through the canyon with the rescued team on board. Lake, Kemper, and the others heaved a collective sigh of relief.

Suddenly, and without warning, O'Donnell's aircraft was hit—most likely by a ground-based rocket—and exploded in flames. Raining parts, the helicopter's momentum carried it forward several hundred yards through the air before it crashed deep into the canyon somewhere beneath the jungle canopy.

After a moment of stunned disbelief, Captain Michael Jimison, one of the Panther pilots, radioed that he would go in for a closer look at the crash site. Since the Cobras were faster helicopters, he was able to pass through the valley at a speed of close to 200 knots. As he made the pass, the canyon walls lit up with muzzle flashes and tracer rounds. From the northern wall of the canyon, Lake saw a white streak of another rocket flash behind the lead Cobra before exploding against the far wall of the canyon. At the end of the run, Jimison reported that he could see nothing in the heavy jungle of the valley floor except for smoke and fire.

A moment later, a massive explosion followed by a dense cloud of black smoke arose from the crash site. Fires were now burning furiously all around the downed helicopter. Lake decided to make a closer investigation of the area himself. He ordered the other gunships and slicks to remain in high orbit while he descended through a veil of smoke toward the crash site. As he slowly circled down into the valley, he saw thousands of tracer rounds flash by on all sides of his aircraft. O'Donnell's helicopter had crashed deep into the valley, flanked by steep walls populated by hundreds of enemy soldiers who were now firing on Lake's ship and crew. From their position on the walls of the canyon, the North Vietnamese soldiers were able to shoot down any aircraft attempting to fly through the valley near the crash site.

Lake's friends lay somewhere beneath the thick jungle canopy, enveloped in flames and surrounded by hostile forces. There was nowhere to land, and hovering within firing range was futile. Lake and Kemper agreed that nothing else could be done. From what they were able to see, neither man believed that anyone could have survived the explosion aboard the aircraft or the subsequent 200-foot fall into the jungle. Lake made a maximum power climb out from the valley, reluctantly turned away, and gave the order for the remaining helicopters to return to base at Dak To. The burning fires in the Cambodian jungle receded slowly into the background as they numbly made their way home.

To protect the lives of those under his command, Jim Lake made the difficult decision to leave the site and return to base. Reflecting on the episode 40 years later, he said, "I made the hardest decision of my life. It was a fateful fucking decision. No one ever went back. The war went on, the next day, more war. We carried on."

At the time of the incident, Jim Lake was 19 years old. Even after all the intervening years and the perspective that comes with age, Lake clearly has never forgiven himself. The consequences of his decisions that day remain with him constantly. As the mission commander, he still maintains that he, and not his friend, should have made the extraction of RT Pennsylvania or died on the field of battle in making the attempt. Jim Lake eventually made it home from the war, but he acknowledges that he left something deep inside him behind with his friends in the jungle of Ratanakiri Province.

For all the men involved in the attempted rescue, the loss of O'Donnell, his crew, and the members of RT Pennsylvania was a terrible blow. To have come so close to success in spite of such superior numbers of enemy forces, the intractable and inhospitable terrain, and the exhausted and desperate condition of the men on the ground was especially hard to take. But there was something else that made this one so tragic. It was witnessing such bravery from one of their own, while they remained so close but unable to help. Upon returning to base, pilot Jonny Kemper said, "It was the most heroic act I have ever seen."

PART TWO

They went with songs to the battle, they were young,
Straight of limb, true of eye, steady and aglow.
They were staunch to the end against odds
    uncounted,
They fell with their faces to the foe.

They shall not grow old, as we that are left grow old:
Age shall not weary them, not the years condemn.
At the going down of the sun and in the morning
We will remember them.

                —FROM "FOR THE FALLEN,"
                    by Laurence Binyon, 1914

Chapter 5

LEFT BEHIND

They woke me this morning
to tell me my brother had been killed in battle.
Yet in the garden
a new rose, with moist petals uncurling, blooms on the bush.
And I am alive,
still breathing the fragrance of roses and dung,
eating, praying, and sleeping.
When can I break my long silence?
When can I speak the unuttered words that are choking me?
— THICH NHAT HANH, *"Peace"*[1]

The next few days were a blur for Lake, Kemper, and the others who had witnessed the tragic events in the Cambodian jungle. As mission commander, Jim Lake had to complete an after action report outlining the sequence of events that day leading to the loss of helicopter and crew. Although he knew exactly where the helicopter had been shot down, Lake recognized that there would be no further search of the crash site given the remote location of the mission and strong presence of the enemy throughout the region. Others turned to the grim task of gathering their friends' belongings to be shipped home.

On Saturday morning, four days after the crash, two uniformed army officers arrived at the O'Donnell home in Springfield, Illinois, to deliver a telegram. Colonel Forestall and his aide informed the O'Donnells that their son had been reported missing. The message in the telegram was terse and inconclusive:

> The Secretary of the Army has asked me to inform you that your son Captain Michael D. O'Donnell has been reported missing in Southeast Asia since 24 March 1970. He was last seen while aircraft commander of a military aircraft on a military mission when the aircraft crashed and burned for unknown reason. Search is in progress. You will be promptly advised when further information is received. In order to protect any information that might be used to your son's detriment your cooperation is requested in making public only information concerning his name, rank, service number, and date of birth. Please accept my deepest sympathy during this most trying period. This confirms personal notification by a representative of the Secretary of the Army.

Although the colonel was polite and highly respectful, he had little else to say, and couldn't answer any of Bette and Don's questions. He recited army procedure and next steps. He explained that an investigation was underway and that they would be informed about progress along the way. But reassurance—that he could not give them. He offered his personal condolences, and departed. In the space of just a few moments the O'Donnells' world had been shattered.

Bette and Don remained standing at the doorway, stunned and paralyzed. Without any real information, they were left to imagine all the dreadful possibilities: that Michael was lost somewhere in a remote land and lay gravely injured, or that he had been captured and was being tortured by the enemy, or that he had been killed in a helicopter crash or an explosion of fire. In the next hours and days, they simply could not come to terms with the ominous message in the telegram, and were at a loss as to what to do next. Like all families informed that a loved one has been listed as missing in action, they had been dropped into an abyss of paralyzing uncertainty without even the cold comfort that they would some day receive answers.

They contacted Patsy, then living in Milwaukee; she returned home that afternoon. They felt an intense need to do something, to take action, but didn't know what action to take. For lack of any better idea, they began notifying other family and friends, although there was little they could tell them. For the next several days the house was filled with visitors who brought distraction, meals, emotional support, and offers to help in any way possible. For Patsy, just waiting for further word from the army was simply unacceptable. She leapt into action, first learning more about the status of MIAs in Vietnam, and then reaching out to her contacts in government in the hope that someone might offer help or advice.

The next morning, Easter Sunday, Patsy shared the news with Marcus Sullivan, who was now attending graduate school in Whitewater. He and his wife, Charlotte, were both devastated to learn that their friend had become a casualty of the war. Later that day Marcus resorted to music to deal with his feelings, composing a song for his friend:

> Woke up this morning, saw you lying there beside me
> and I felt your breath upon my face.
> I heard the sound of the telephone bell, and I said oh well,
> it was time to get up anyway.
> The word came down on Easter morn'
> that he was gone and you know that
> I was glad not to be alone.
> He was my friend . . .

Years later, Marcus remembered vividly that he felt "shock, uncertainty, and numbness, but also hope and fear that he might be hurt, captured, or mistreated if he had survived."

The wait for more information wasn't long. Colonel Forestall returned the following Tuesday evening to deliver a second telegram. The updated message was even more bleak, delivered in the bureaucratic language of the army:

> I regret to inform you that additional information received
> from the oversea commander concerning your son Captain
> Michael D. O'Donnell states that efforts to reach the crash site
> of the aircraft on which your son was the commander have
> not been successful because of intervention by hostile forces

in the area. The search is continuing. In those instances where a member's fate is not definitely ascertained the circumstances surrounding his disappearance are thoroughly investigated. Our regulations require the organization commander to convene a Board of Officers to conduct the investigation within ten days after the incident.

The Board will examine all available evidence, interrogate associates and those who can contribute information which will assist them in arriving at a sound and logical conclusion. The Board may recommend a change in Michael's status to deceased should the evidence be adequately conclusive to support such a finding. However, in the absence of conclusive evidence it is normal that he be continued as missing. The report of the proceeding of this Board of Officers should be in my office within 60 days. However, I will correspond with you again during the month of May 1970 and, of course, should any new developments occur I shall inform you immediately.

With these two telegrams, the O'Donnell family began their official correspondence with the US Army, an arduous and dispiriting process that was to continue without interruption for more than 30 years.

The day after the O'Donnells received the second telegram, Jane received a hand-delivered message while she was in class at Florida State, requesting that she return home. When she arrived, she found her father seated in the living room. With tears in his eyes, he told her that the O'Donnells had just called to tell them that Mike had been shot down while on a mission in a remote location somewhere in the Central Highlands of Vietnam. Although Jane can no longer remember exactly what she was told that day, she does remember the gist of it: Mike's helicopter had been attacked, it had exploded, and he was lost. It was clear to her that Mike had been killed. As she said many years later, at that moment, she just knew.

Like the O'Donnells, Jane had been living each day since Mike had left with the fear that he would become a casualty of this ghastly war. She had asked him so many times to avoid being a hero, to be careful and come home to her. He always assured her that he would, and then he'd quickly change the subject. Although he never specifically reported on the war in his letters, Jane had noticed that he seemed increasingly downcast and dispirited by his bleak circumstances. Nonetheless, the fear that he would die had not prepared her to receive the news that he was actually gone, lost without a trace somewhere on the other side of the world, engulfed by what seemed to her a thoroughly pointless and cruel war. It just made no sense. The loss of Michael devastated her. She had been enrolled in graduate school at Florida State, working on an MA and teaching Portuguese while she awaited Michael's return, their marriage, and a new life together. Now she felt lost and completely alone. By the end of the term, in the spring of 1970, Jane withdrew from graduate school to move to Brazil, where she planned to teach English at Catholic University in Rio de Janeiro and disappear from her world for a while. Jane's family had lived in Rio in 1967 and 1968, while her father served with USAID; she had visited while in college and had family friends there who could keep an eye on her. By getting away from the constant presence of the war and everything else that was familiar, Jane would have time and space to grieve and figure out the rest of her life, or at least what to do next. She left for Rio in the summer of 1970 with a plan to remain for one year.

BACK IN KONTUM, Mike's comrades had no time to reflect on what had happened. The relentless grind of the war continued, each day bringing yet another mission and new terrors. The arduous demands of the war paradoxically helped them to get through it. Grieving and reflection would come later, after the war, when there would be a great deal of time finally to absorb all that had happened to them. Right now they needed to focus on supporting each other and doing what was required to survive another day.

They did, however, have to perform the grim ritual of gathering Mike's personal effects for shipment home to his family. As they were searching his footlocker, they found a portable typewriter and, beneath it, a collection of poems that had been gathered into a file labeled *Letters from Pleiku*. Although everyone knew that Mike had been writing poetry, he had not talked about it much, and no one had read anything he had written. Now, reading his work, they were deeply moved. The poems spoke directly to them about their own experiences and the grim reality they faced every day in this distant and terrible place, so far from everything and everyone they loved. Mike's friends made copies and distributed them around the base. Soon the poems began to circulate more widely, from base to base throughout Vietnam.

An English journalist named Bryan Benton, who was at the time attached to Mike's unit in Kontum, brought a copy of the poems home with him when he returned to London a few months later.

Within days of the O'Donnell incident, Jim Lake and the other members of the 170th were back in their helicopters flying missions into the mountainous terrain of North Vietnam, Cambodia, and Laos, although it hardly mattered where they were being sent. The war was always the same, wherever and whenever it was being fought. As Jim Lake described:

> We got up at 5:00am every day, first we went to the mess hall, then to the flight line, and then flew from Kontum to Dak To, where we waited around for our orders to engage the enemy. We saw action every single day. Then we went back to Kontum early evening, usually in time to watch the missile attacks on our base, which also occured every single day. Following that we would have dinner and then drink at the bar until about midnight. The next day we would do it all over again.

In the middle of this routine, people were being injured and killed in and around their helicopters on a daily basis. One pilot in Lake's unit reported that, on a single mission, his ship had been hit by gunfire 54 times.

On April 15, the unit was shaken by another battle with significant losses. In the midst of heavy fighting in the mountains just north of the base at Dak To, Roger Miller, a pilot who had joined the unit only one week earlier, crashed on the field of battle as he attempted to rescue fellow soldiers and the crew from another downed helicopter. Miller's ship was ambushed as it was taking passengers. Despite a broken leg and gunshot wounds to his hand and arm, Miller escaped into the jungle, managing to evade capture until the next morning. Everyone else on board was killed. Over the course of the next several months, Miller had his shattered thumb amputated by an enemy medic and, for lack of better options, improvised the treatment of his gangrenous arm by allowing maggots to eat away the infection as he was slowly marched to Hanoi. Miller would remain a POW until March 1973, when the American government negotiated his release as a condition of ending US involvement in the war.

On April 30, President Nixon announced the invasion of Cambodia, which was certainly no surprise to the members of the 170th, who had been flying missions there for several months. Whatever the military justification for extending the war into Cambodia, the reaction at home was explosive, resulting in rallies and protests across the country, but especially on college campuses. Four days later, at Kent State in Ohio, members of the National Guard killed four students and wounded nine others while attempting to suppress a student demonstration. Yet, for all the drama and controversy about the war at home, for the men continuing on in Kontum, the issues of presidential policies, military strategy, or even national politics were of little moment and never the subject of discussion. Never. As Jim Lake said, "We were in a small, dangerous place in the middle of nowhere. We had little access to information about the world or even the war. We tried to get through each day and take care of each other. We fought that war for our buddies, and that was it."

In the summer of 1970, the members of the 170th Assault Helicopter Company were informed that they should prepare for the deactivation of their unit as President Nixon's policy of "Vietnamization" was resulting in the gradual drawdown of US troops. The unit, activated in September 1965, had within five years achieved a distinguished record of service in Vietnam with numerous citations and awards, as well as a record of 58 dead and many more wounded. By February 1971, George Crawford, the final commander of the 170th, decided to move the unit back to Camp Holloway in Pleiku since they no longer had sufficient numbers of men and were increasingly short of equipment and supplies to be able to fly their helicopters safely. One month later, exactly a year after Michael O'Donnell had been shot down, the 170th Assault Helicopter Company was finally deactivated.

Journalist Bryan Benton, who had returned to London with a copy of O'Donnell's poems, had been sharing them with numerous colleagues. One of them was Ian Brodie, a colleague working for the *London Sunday Express*. In March of 1972, Brodie published 14 of O'Donnell's poems in the paper, along with his own account of O'Donnell's poetry and its impact on his fellow soldiers. Brodie wrote that "O'Donnell had brilliantly captured the familiar American sufferings in Vietnam of frustration, fear, loneliness, and yearning to be home with a great economy of words." He went on to say that the poems "are becoming something of a cult in Vietnam. Increasingly, they are being copied, passed around, and read aloud by pilots and others who discover their own thoughts and experiences sharply etched in O'Donnell's simple statements."[2]

After the poems were published, interest in them continued to rise. Later that year, several American newspapers included his poems in their Memorial Day editions, usually adding a brief description of the author and his uncertain fate in Vietnam. By the end of the war in 1975, Michael O'Donnell's poems were widely distributed and increasingly well known, especially among veterans. He was being remembered as a war poet of importance, even if his status as a soldier missing in action remained uncertain.

NIXON'S VIETNAMIZATION POLICY had by 1973 led to the complete withdrawal of all US troops from Vietnam. There had been 475,000 American troops deployed when he was inaugurated in 1969; by 1971 there were 156,800, and a year later only 24,200. The wind down of troops meant that during the last few years of the war, a small group of undersupplied and vastly outnumbered soldiers had to close out the war on a timetable and with resources determined by politicians who soldiers recognized to be, for the most part, dishonest and unconcerned about their well-being. As writer and Vietnam veteran Larry Heinemann wrote, "And if it is true that two-thirds of the US troops in Viet Nam were volunteers, it is also true that we learned of our betrayal as soon as we set foot in the field. The war was a shuck, as the saying goes, and ordinary soldiers understood well enough that we had been fucked—to say it clearly and unmistakably." Heinemann went on to say more directly what all the soldiers came to understand clearly by the last years of the war, namely that "the government would rather kill us all than admit a mistake."[3] Most of the 4,700 soldiers who died in Vietnam after Michael O'Donnell did were aware that the cause they had been fighting for was a "shuck" and that, in any event, the war had actually been lost long ago. The policy of Vietnamization was clearly not about peace with honor, as Nixon had proclaimed; it was rather a cynical political maneuver to transfer accountability for the inevitable defeat to the hapless and incompetent government of the South before it was too late. In April 1975, the Republic of Vietnam finally succumbed to the Communists, leaving the last few Americans in Saigon to flee in helicopters awaiting them on the roof of the American embassy and elsewhere in the city. As these last Americans scrambled to the embassy roof and the safety of the naval ships awaiting them offshore, they could see below in the receding distance their Vietnamese colleagues and friends who had supported them for so long, left behind to confront an ominous fate at the hands of a harsh and vindictive enemy.

At the time of the final defeat, there remained in Vietnam some 2,500 American soldiers listed as missing in action.[4] For the time being, they too had been left behind. The American people and especially their government were desperate to move on. Coverage of the Vietnam War and its aftermath simply disappeared from the news. Stories of the soldiers who had fought in the war and were now struggling to return to normal life were simply not told. Even popular music had abandoned the war. While the folk scene in the 1960s championed the peace movement as it actively protested the war, by 1974, only a single song in the top 100 was about war, and that was the insipid "Billy Don't Be a Hero" by Bo Donaldson and the Heywoods, which was, in any event, about the Civil War. After nearly 15 years of national attention and ex-cruciating national debate, the Vietnam story had exhausted the American people. Finally, Democrats and Republicans, hippies and radicals, conservatives and liberals, all agreed on something about the Vietnam War: it was time to change the subject and move on.

During the years after Mike's disappearance, the O'Donnells continued to receive reports from the army—generally several a year—updating them on his MIA status. The letters, issued perhaps with the best intentions, albeit in a mechanistic and bu-reaucratic manner, were devoid of new information, or much of anything that was helpful. For the O'Donnells, these letters were nothing more than a series of painful reminders of what they had lost. As Bette wrote to Marcus in August 1971, notwithstanding the many reports the family had received, "There's been no news of our boy. We've done everything we can think of—to no avail."

In 1978, after eight years without evidence of progress of any kind, the O'Donnell family formally requested that Michael's status be changed to killed in action. The war was long over, and the government-issued reports had not presented a single piece of encouraging news or, for that matter, any evidence indi-cating that Mike had survived the crash. By changing his status, the family could achieve some semblance of closure, even if it meant formally ending Mike's record of active service and the salary that continued to be paid into his account. At the time his status was changed to deceased, Michael O'Donnell was post-humously promoted to major before the family was issued his honorable discharge papers.

Don O'Donnell died in 1987, never having learned what had happened to his son. Some years later, Bette succumbed to Alzheimer's, and then died in 2003. Mike's parents never learned anything more about the fate of their son than had been provided to them in the two telegrams they received in March 1970.

Chapter 6

AFTERMATH

When the war has ended and the road is open again,
the same stars will course through the heavens.
Then will I weep for the white bones heaped together in
    desolate graves
of those who sought military honors for their leaders.
                —FROM THE DIARY OF AN UNKNOWN
                NORTH VIETNAMESE SOLDIER, 1965[1]

Let us remember Spring will come again
To the scorched, blackened woods, where
    the wounded trees
Wait with their old wise patience for the heavenly
    rain,
Sure of the sky: sure of the sea to send its healing
    breeze,
Sure of the sun. And even as to these
Surely the spring, when God shall please,
Will come again like a divine surprise
To those who sit to-day with their great Dead, hands in
    their hands, eyes in their eyes,
At one with Love, at one with Grief: blind to the
    scattered things and changing skies.
                —CHARLOTTE MEW, *May 1915*[2]

With the end of hostilities and the inevitable defeat of the Republic of Vietnam—and by extension the United States—the final chapter of the war had finally been written, at least so far as most Americans knew. The 11-year period from the Gulf of Tonkin Resolution in August of 1964 to the capture of the American embassy in Saigon in April 1975 was among the most consequential in the nation's history, and it was certainly one of the most painful. As had been the case during the Civil War era, the country had found itself deeply divided over a moral issue of defining importance: in the case of the Civil War, by the question of how a democracy ostensibly dedicated to liberty in the age of the so-called Enlightenment could continue to enslave fellow human beings; and in the case of Vietnam, by the question of what, beyond self-defense, constitutes a legitimate basis to wage war—sacrificing others in service of a political idea—and by whose authority such decisions should be made. In both cases the wars themselves did not fully resolve the moral issues they raised.[3] As divided as the nation was about the moral or political "rightness" of American involvement in Vietnam, in the immediate aftermath of the war, there was increasing agreement across the political spectrum that the strategy of containment had failed and that waging war in service of a political agenda was simply immoral.[4] As William Greider wrote in the *Washington Post* in April 1975, the week after the fall of Saigon, "The years of false predictions, unfilled political promises and deceitful claims of progress left an awful legacy of cynicism and distrust, which will blight politics and foreign policy for many years."[5]

In the weeks and months following US withdrawal from the war, the American people asserted in myriad ways that the mistakes of Vietnam must not happen again. Across the country and the political spectrum, Americans declared that they would no longer tolerate sacrificing their own citizens in military conflicts where goals were poorly defined and progress difficult to measure beyond the ugly math of body counts. The human trauma of the Vietnam War was difficult to absorb, as was the loss of clarity about what constituted an acceptable foreign policy. After nearly two centuries of American military success, most recently in the Second World War, first the stalemate in Korea and then the massive failure in Vietnam challenged the government's understanding of what constituted effective interventionist policy; it became increasingly clear that the American people would not accept or even tolerate military incursions without a compelling case and clear evidence of consultation across branches of government and with the public.

After the spectacular failure of Richard Nixon's presidency, followed by Gerald Ford's controversial decision to pardon the disgraced president, and the final loss of Vietnam to the Communists in 1975, the election of Jimmy Carter in 1976 promised a new era of government characterized by honesty and ethically grounded leadership. Americans wanted to look ahead and forget the recent past, which was, as American scholar and critic Marita Sturken described, "too dangerous to keep in active memory."[6] But moving past the Vietnam era would not be easy. The losses had been too great, the benefits too few, and most important, the people who had suffered and sacrificed for the war were simply too numerous. The nation was about to learn that it simply could not walk away. Journalist and historian Garry Wills made this point in an editorial a few weeks after the final US withdrawal, "There is nothing more interesting about our collapse and withdrawal from Vietnam than the injunction that we should not allow ourselves to think about it. . . . It would be suicidal for any organization or individual to forbid study of its own experience, especially an experience of setback or defeat."[7]

The numbers alone were just too large to ignore. If in 1964 the United States was engaged in a fairly modest military venture in a remote country of questionable global importance, by the end of that "venture," 58,220 American soldiers had been killed and another 150,000 wounded, of whom 75,000 were severely disabled. During this period the United States had dropped seven million tons of bombs on both enemy combatants and innocent civilians throughout Vietnam, as well as in Cambodia and Laos. In all, the US bombing in this war exceeded that of World War II—both European and Pacific theaters—and Korea combined. The resulting losses to the Vietnamese were staggering, including more than two million dead, countless wounded, and the near obliteration of the country itself.

The economic cost was also substantial, beginning with the direct US expenditure of $600 billion. Whatever else might have been achieved, and it is not at all clear that anything meaningfully good had been achieved, the war categorically failed to contain the spread of communism farther into Southeast Asia. Perhaps most remarkably, the American politicians and strategists who supported the war and guided its progress had never come to understand, or at least they did not take seriously, that for Ho Chi Minh and those who followed him, the conflict was part of a long-standing struggle for independence, not a referendum on communism.

Beyond the hard costs, there were the costs more elusive and difficult to measure, including especially the impact of the war on the 2.7 million American soldiers who served in Vietnam, and among them, the 750,000 who survived nearly continuous combat conditions. Many who served returned home to face a wide range of physical and psychological challenges, which soon proved to be persistent and remained poorly understood. In large part because the nation was so eager to turn the page on the war, the veterans' problems—what we now recognize to be clear evidence of post-traumatic stress disorder (PTSD)—were actively neglected by the very government that had imposed the trauma on them in the first place.[8] But the American people didn't have any idea about what lay ahead for these Vietnam veterans, either. It soon became clear that for many of them, recovery would not be easy or even possible.

For those who served in Vietnam, the experience of war was dramatically different from what American soldiers had faced before. As historian Marc Jason Gilbert describes:

> Many of these soldiers saw a face of battle that was particularly harsh. It mated close-quarter guerilla warfare with unprecedented conventional firepower capable of butchering combatants and noncombatants, friends and foes alike. On the other hand, it witnessed advances in medical services that ensured that all but the most seriously wounded could be quickly

returned to the killing ground. . . . These young soldiers often initially engaged opponents as part of small units operating at enormous numerical disadvantage, where survival depended on a high degree of mutual trust and reliance between individuals. Yet these crucial intimate relationships were undermined by the one-year rotation system and high casualty rates.[9]

Of course, beyond these challenges, veterans had to reconcile their personal sacrifices against what most now acknowledged had been both a morally unjustified and a losing effort. To make matters worse, as John Wheeler, cofounder of the Vietnam Veterans Memorial, wrote in the *New York Times*, they "encountered a social taboo that in effect decreed the most searing experience of their lives was not to be discussed."[10]

This climate of apparent indifference to their experiences—medically, psychologically, and personally—fostered myriad problems for the returning veterans who were struggling to find their way back into society. These included depression, substance abuse, suicide, homelessness, and numerous other psychological problems now attributed to PTSD. To be sure, simply moving on was not going to be possible with so many still struggling to make sense of what had happened to them and more generally to their country.

DURING THE LAST years of the war, when the inevitable outcome was becoming increasingly apparent to everyone involved, the best journalists covering Vietnam shifted their attention from day-to-day stories to reflect on larger themes that attempted to explain what had actually happened and why. Two of the most successful of these works, both published in 1972, were *Fire in the Lake* by Frances FitzGerald and *The Best and the Brightest* by David Halberstam. FitzGerald, who received the Pulitzer Prize, the National Book Award, and the Bancroft Prize for her book, wrote that it was intended to be a "first draft of history." In providing a deep historical and cultural reading of Vietnam, FitzGerald was the first to argue that the Americans had limited real knowledge of the country they were invading and a generally poor conception of the Vietnamese people—who saw the conflict not as a means of liberating them from the yoke of communism, but rather as another effort at colonial subjugation. Halberstam, by contrast, set out to understand American leadership, and particularly how the "best and the brightest" could have been so wrong in Vietnam. Both books were widely praised, paving the way for a more historically nuanced understanding of the political moment, the key players, and the reasons behind the many mistakes that came to define the war. FitzGerald, Halberstam, and a number of other writers helped to generate a new kind of interest in a subject so many wanted to leave behind.

Important though these books were, they did little to help veterans and their families to cope with the personal consequences of the war. As Philip Caputo has written, "By the mid-1970s, the public had heard enough about Vietnam from journalists, commentators, and analysts of every kind. . . . Vietnam was considered a legitimate subject for journalism, but as a subject for literature it was almost as taboo as explicit sex had been to the

Victorians."[11] But veterans and many others still had a strong desire to reflect on what the experience meant to those who did the fighting and dying. Caputo, who had served two tours of duty in Vietnam, felt a need to connect outsiders, especially those he characterized as the self-righteous critics of the war, more directly to what had happened. In his first book, the memoir *A Rumor of War*, which was published in 1977, Caputo strove

> to make people uncomfortable—in effect, to blow them out of their snug polemical bunkers into the confusing, disturbing emotional and moral no-man's-land where we warriors dwelled. . . . I did not want to *tell* anyone about the war but to *show* it. I wanted readers to feel the heat, the monsoons, the mosquitoes, to experience the snipers, booby traps, and ambushes. Above all, I wanted to communicate the moral ambiguities of a conflict in which demons and angels traded places too often to tell one from the other, even within yourself.[12]

During these early postwar years, along with Caputo's work, a new wave of important writing about Vietnam began to appear that focused on the lived experience of the soldier. The emphasis in these works—memoirs, novels, and poetry—was on the *personal experience* of those doing the fighting and dying, rather than the politics, history, or even military strategy of the war. In books by Tim O'Brien, Larry Heinemann, Michael Herr, and Ron Kovic among others, war writing progressed beyond frontline journalistic accounts to give voice to the soldiers themselves.[13] Those who had done the fighting, suffering, and dying, and those who had been left behind, were emerging as a crucial part of the story of the war itself.

Ron Kovic was among the first veterans to write a major memoir of the war, *Born on the Fourth of July*, published in 1976. Kovic, who had enlisted in the Marines in 1964 and was a self-styled patriot and a strong supporter of the war, served two tours in Vietnam before suffering a catastrophic injury in 1968, which resulted in paralysis from the chest down. During the long ordeal of his recovery, and then following the Kent State killings, Kovic's position changed, and he became one of the most active veterans protesting against the war. In writing his memoir, Kovic later explained:

> I wanted people to understand. I wanted to share with them as nakedly and openly and intimately as possible what I had gone through, what I had endured. I wanted them to know what it really meant to be in a war—to be shot and wounded, to be fighting for my life on the intensive care ward—not the myth we had grown up believing. I wanted people to know about the hospitals and the enema room, about why I had become opposed to the war, why I had grown more and more committed to peace and nonviolence.[14]

The distinctive character of the Vietnam War also produced a great deal of poetry, comparable in quantity if perhaps not always in quality to the work of the great soldier poets of Britain in the First World War. Those poets were unequaled in capturing the grueling and appalling conditions of trench warfare as well as the psychological state of individuals pushed beyond the limits of human endurance through protracted exposure to inconceivable cruelty and hardship. Among the finest of these was Siegfried Sassoon, who often explored the sharp contrast between popular rhetoric about the war and the very different reality for the soldiers, as he did in the 1916 poem "They":

> The Bishop tells us: 'When the boys come back
> They will not be the same; for they'll have fought
> In a just cause: they lead the last attack
> On Anti-Christ; their comrades' blood had bought
> New right to breed an honorable race,
> They have challenged Death and dared him face to face.'
>
> 'We're none of us the same!' the boys reply.
> 'For George lost both his legs; and Bill's stone blind;
> Poor Jim's shot through his lungs and like to die;
> And Bert's gone syphilitic: you'll not find
> A chap who's served that hasn't found *some* change.'
> And the Bishop said; 'The ways of God are strange!'

In his poem "Grotesque," Frederic Manning, like Sassoon, wrote of the terrible contradiction between the lofty ideology and ugly reality that all soldiers inevitably had to face once they were on the battlefield or in the trench:

> These are the damned circles Dante trod,
> Terrible in hopelessness,
> But even skulls have their humor,
> An eyeless and sardonic mockery;
> And we,
> Sitting with streaming eyes in the acrid smoke,

That murks our foul, damp billet,
Chant bitterly, with raucous voices
As a choir of frogs
In hideous irony, our patriotic songs.

The soldier poets of Vietnam also explored the grim reality and emotional experience of their particular war. As W. D. Ehrhart has observed, not all the work from Vietnam is highly accomplished from a literary standpoint, but it offered a voice for "soldiers so hurt and bitter that they could not maintain their silence any longer."[15] Like Michael O'Donnell, many of the war poets of the Vietnam era were young volunteers who accepted the premise that they were entering a conflict deserving of their commitment and sacrifice. When they discovered otherwise, usually after they had become trapped inside the war with no chance for escape, some of these soldiers resorted to poetry to express what they were experiencing, which somehow they could not communicate in any other way. Clearly, the combination of loneliness and sense of betrayal that so many of these poets experienced was a central component of their work. As Ehrhart described, "each soldier went to Vietnam alone and unheralded, and those who survived came home alone to an alien land—indifferent or even hostile to them—where the war continued to rage no farther away than the nearest television set or newspaper, or the nearest street demonstration."[16]

Many of the themes expressed in the work of these poets echo one another, but the perspectives offered by the best of them can be distinct and startling. In the poem "Morning—A Death," Basil Paquet, a conscientious objector who served as a combat medic in Vietnam, writes with extraordinary force about the moment of death for a soldier on the battlefield, at least as it was experienced by a combat medic:

> I've blown up your chest for thirty minutes
> And crushed it down an equal time
> And still you won't warm to my kisses
> I've sucked and puffed on your
> Metal No. 8 throat for so long,
> And twice you've moaned under my thrusts
> On your breastbone. I've worn off
> Those sparse hairs you counted noble on your chest,
> And twice you defibrillated,
> And twice blew back my breath.
>
> You are dead just as finally
> As your mucosity dries on my lips
> In this morning sun.
> I have thumped and blown into your kind too often.
> I grow tired of kissing the dead.[17]

Paquet's poem invites us to contemplate what death on the field of battle actually looks and feels like for a medic. By contrast, John Balaban, a conscientious objector who served in Vietnam as a volunteer for an NGO, provides a deeply disturbing image of what being left behind actually means in his masterful "In Celebration of Spring":

> Our Asian war is over; others have begun.
> Our elders, who tried to mortgage lies,
> are disgraced, or dead, and already
> the brokers are picking their pockets
> for the keys and the credit cards.

In a delta swamp in a united Vietnam,
a Marine with a bullfrog for a face
rots in equatorial heat. An eel
slides through the cage of his bared ribs.
At night, on the still battlefields, ghosts,
like patches of fog, lurk into villages
to maunder on doorsills or cratered homes,
while all across the U.S. in this 200th year
of revolution and the rights of man,
the wounded walk about and wonder where to go.

And today, in the simmer of lyric sunlight,
a chrysalis pulses in its mushy cocoon
under the bark on a gnarled root of an elm.
In the brilliant creek, a minnow flashes
delirious with gnats. The turtle's heart
quickens its taps in the warm bank sludge.
As she chases a Frisbee spinning in sunlight
a girl's breasts bounce full and strong;
a boy's stomach, as he turns, is flat and strong.

Swear by the locust, by dragonflies on ferns,
by the minnow's flash, the tremble of a breast,
by the new earth spongy under our feet:
that as we grow old, we will not grow evil,
that although our garden seeps with sewage,
and our elders think it's up for auction—swear
by this dazzle that does not wish to leave us—
that we will be keepers of a garden, nonetheless.[18]

In contrasting a dead marine with an attractive young couple playing with a Frisbee on a bountiful spring day, Balaban provokes us to reflect, not only on the persistence of loss, but on the grue-some tragedy of untimely death in war. He also seeks to remind us of what is at stake as we grow old. If, as Laurence Binyon observes, the dead "shall not grow old, as we that are left grow old," Balaban asks the generation that survived Vietnam, through the passing of time not to become like their elders who betrayed them.

LIKE THOSE OF Paquet and Balaban, the poems of Michael O'Donnell make important contributions to our understanding of the war, and especially the emotional side of the surreal world the poets inhabited. They focus on the themes of loneliness, loss, and the interior life of a helicopter pilot who had almost daily ex-posure to death, but spent each evening back at the base, enacting a wearying routine that eroded his spirit and seemed gradually to prepare him for his own death. Given the sadness found in his po-ems and his destiny in Vietnam, O'Donnell's life was ultimately tragic. But he would no doubt find it redemptive that his poems came to be widely embraced, especially by those who had served and whose inner lives connected so fully with his own.

With the rise of this new interest in the veteran's experience, as recounted in memoirs, novels, and poems, there also emerged a new genre of films that explored the personal consequences of war on veterans and their families. *Coming Home* and *The Deer Hunter* were among the best of these early films. Both released in 1978 to critical acclaim, these films each in its own way offered an honest but sympathetic examination of damaged people trying to rebuild their lives under difficult circumstances. In *Coming Home* the damage to Vietnam vet Luke Martin was physical, and in *Deer Hunter* the three friends, all who suffered greatly in the war, deal with PTSD and grave physical injuries.

These films and others that came later offered a mass audience a new understanding of a war they had not experienced—both the fury of battle and its traumatic aftermath. Of course, no experience in a theater, accompanied by popcorn and a soft drink, can give the viewer even a remote sense of the trauma and sheer terror of battle, or for that matter, its impact over time. But viewed as a collective enterprise, literature, historical writing, poetry, and film have contributed a great deal to our understanding of war from perspectives that would otherwise be unavailable.

After seeing *The Deer Hunter*, a film he believed to be both honest and sympathetic to the trauma faced by those who fought in Vietnam, a young veteran named Jan Scruggs founded the Vietnam Veterans Memorial Fund and pitched the idea for a memorial on the National Mall—one that would specifically honor veterans' sacrifices rather than the cause, the conflict, or its leaders. There was initially little public support for the idea, but the Vietnam Veterans Memorial Fund began to receive support from influential veterans serving in Congress and elsewhere, and shortly thereafter the movement had raised the necessary funds and, even more impressive, secured approval to build a memorial on the National Mall adjacent to the Lincoln Memorial. President Jimmy Carter signed the order for this memorial in July 1980.

At the time, the design selected for the memorial was controversial. The architect, Maya Lin, a young Asian American college student and nonveteran had proposed a radical departure from the heroic conventions of earlier war memorials. Occupying two acres of land on the National Mall, the memorial consists of two highly polished black granite walls that recede into the earth from their point of intersection at the center. The names of more than 58,300 dead and missing American soldiers are inscribed on the highly reflective surface along the entire 500-foot length of the memorial. The horizontal orientation and unobtrusive silhouette of the memorial wall drew criticism from those who felt that a minimalist memorial would not sufficiently honor the sacrifices of those who died.[19] Yet Lin's design was consistent with the specifications set forth for the competition, which called for a memorial that would "harmonize with its surroundings" and "make no political statement about the war."[20] Although her design was not explicitly political, the placement of the memorial on the National Mall, so close to the location of the many anti-war protests, was itself seen as a political gesture.[21]

The dedication of the Vietnam Veterans Memorial in November 1982 represented a major turning point in how Americans thought about the war, in particular by helping them to distinguish between, on the one hand, the moral and ethical issues associated with America's policies in Vietnam and, on the other, the profound sacrifice of individuals called upon to fight the war. Although the memorial was at first highly controversial, its impact was profound and almost entirely unanticipated. For many Americans seeking a way to express their feelings about the war and their empathy for those who suffered through it, the new memorial came to serve as a *locus sanctus*. It quickly became one of the most frequently visited sites in Washington, and remains so today. One of the most surprising responses to the new memorial—which began at the very outset—was the practice of leaving objects at the wall, ranging from everyday items to deeply personal gifts to war-related relics. Kristin Hass argued that for many the site "captures the unlikely simultaneous experiences of reflection and burial," functioning as both a memorial and a collective headstone.[22]

Shortly after the memorial was dedicated, the Parks and History Association published a commemorative volume entitled *Let Us Remember: The Vietnam Veterans Memorial*, which provided a historical overview on the project and outlined the purpose of the memorial. The booklet included a single poem, which was placed on the final page: "If You Are Able" by Michael O'Donnell.

Throughout this process of national reflection and painful debate, and especially following the dedication of the Vietnam Veterans Memorial in Washington, Michael O'Donnell's poetry found increasingly larger audiences among veterans, writers, filmmakers, and the public. Over the next few years, O'Donnell's work would be incorporated into several other memorials around the nation, most notably the Vietnam Veterans Memorial in New York City, but also those in California, Illinois, Kansas, and South Dakota. At the time of its dedication in New York in May 1985, the Memorial Commission stated that the memorial "should express reconciliation and an awareness of the enduring human values which are reflected in the conflicting experiences of the Vietnam war." Some years later, Bernard Edelman, who had led the effort to create the New York Vietnam Veterans Memorial, described O'Donnell's poem "If You Are Able" as the "anthem poem for Vietnam veterans."[23]

Following the terrorist attacks of September 11, 2001, Michael O'Donnell's work found a new audience when his poem "If You Are Able" was included in a memorial volume published to honor the New York City police and firefighters who had been killed. In the five decades since Michael O'Donnell wrote this poem from his remote base in the Central Highlands of Vietnam, his prophetic call for reconciliation has become a treasured legacy of the war.

Chapter 7

RECOVERY

In the jungle of years,
lost voices are calling. Long
are the memories,
bitterly long the waiting,
and the names of the missing and dead
wander
disembodied
through a green tangle
of rumors and lies,
gliding like shadows among vines.

—W. D. EHRHART, POW/MIA[1]

While the initiative to recover, identify, and repatriate the remains of American war dead began in the early years of the nineteenth century—during the Seminole Wars of Florida—this practice became official policy during the Civil War when fallen soldiers, both Union and Confederate, remained unburied and largely abandoned across the American landscape.[2] The first significant attempts to assign responsibility for properly tending to the fallen were issued in the form of War Department General Orders of 1861 and 1862; General Order No. 33, issued in April 1862, for example, designated primary responsibility for the recovery and identification of combat fatalities to the commander on the field of battle. The military continued to modify these policies to increase their effectiveness throughout the remaining years of the Civil War, but the essential and enduring principle had been established that "public opinion and the armed forces would no longer tolerate the indifference that had heretofore attended the care of the nation's dead in war."[3]

As Drew Faust has observed, while this initiative gained momentum after the end of hostilities:

> Only gradually in the years following southern surrender did a general sense of obligation toward the dead yield firm policy. Only slowly did the orders of individual military commanders combine with legislative authorization and funding to create an enormous and comprehensive postwar reburial program intended to locate every Union soldier across the South and inter all within a new system of national cemeteries. But this was not the goal at the outset. Widespread and continuing public discussion about the dead gradually articulated a set of principles that influenced military and legislative policy.[4]

This obligation to the dead, "a stewardship, the account of which must be rendered," as Walt Whitman described it at the time, was based in part on the fact that the government had conscripted into the army many of those killed in the war, and in doing so incurred a moral obligation to its citizens.[5] Clara Barton, the well-known Civil War nurse, made the point bluntly in a letter to Secretary of War Edwin Stanton: "I hold these men in the light of Government property unaccounted for."[6] With time, as Faust observed, "the transcendent ideals of citizenship, sacrifice, and national obligation united with highly practical and ever-growing concerns . . . to result in what was arguably the most elaborate federal program undertaken in nearly a century of American nationhood."[7]

In the century following the Civil War, in conflicts great and small, the American commitment to the recovery, identification, and burial of its war dead remained a steadfast element of national policy. With time and experience, the nation came to see and appreciate the benefits of such a policy. On the practical side, these included the value forensic evidence provided in helping to explain what actually transpired on the field of battle. For example, in December 1944, a forensic examination of American casualties in Malmedy, France, disclosed that the soldiers had been captured and then massacred by the German SS, not killed in battle.[8] Yet the greatest benefit in maintaining reverence for the dead was for fellow soldiers, who placed the highest importance on the recovery of lost comrades. Given the nature of the human bond that developed between soldiers during wartime, their commitment to each other was, above all else, what sustained them. This was as true for the ancient Greek warriors of the *Iliad* as it was for Wilfred Owen in the First World War and for Jim Lake in Vietnam. In the time of the Vietnam War, the practice of leaving no one behind was considered a creed, just as it was for the Greeks and the Trojans in Homeric times. For all these soldiers, the duty of care extended beyond their living obligations to each other into realms unknown, and they were willing to risk everything to fulfill that duty.

Yet, like so much else concerning the conflict in Vietnam, the problems associated with recovering casualties were unprecedented, and in the early years after the American withdrawal, nearly intractable. The first problem was simple logistics: the Americans did not control the land. Since General Westmoreland's military objective had been to wear down the enemy through "search and destroy" tactics, but not to acquire or control their territory, standard practice was for the Americans to vacate the field of battle as soon as they possessed it. As a result, more often than not the war zone containing American casualties reverted to the enemy. Recovery efforts during the war, such as the one involving Michael O'Donnell's downed helicopter in the Cambodian highlands, were generally ill-fated or even suicidal from the outset. In such circumstances, the dead had to be left where they fell. The second problem was political: because the war effectively ended in a stalemate, or at least without an American victory, there was no immediate basis for any resolution to the problem of MIAs. Moreover, the Vietnamese Communists came to understand that there would be real value in using the MIA issue as a tool in future negotiations. In the decade immediately following the American evacuation of Saigon (1975–1985), there were no attempts to find or recover the remains of the more than 2,500 Americans left behind in Vietnam, Cambodia, and Laos.

Because the war ended under a cloud of controversy, just as it had begun, and because the American people were eager to put it behind them, they also turned away from the problem of finding those who were missing in action. This, they were encouraged to do by President Ford in the days immediately following the evacuation of Saigon in 1975, when he implored Americans "to close ranks, to avoid recrimination about the past, to look ahead to the many goals we share, and to work together on the great tasks that remain to be accomplished."[9] Yet for the families of the missing, like the O'Donnells, looking ahead effectively meant giving up hope; no American presence in Vietnam meant no prospect of closure. Controversial though it was to leave the missing behind, the government's political calculation was that doing so was not an unreasonable concession, since their number was relatively modest compared to those missing in earlier wars. By comparison, 170,000 Union soldiers were never recovered after the Civil War, and at least an equal number of Confederate dead remained missing. Following World War II, 78,000 GIs were unaccounted for, and an additional 8,000 Americans were left behind after the Korean War.[10]

Of course, the desire to move beyond the national trauma of Vietnam was not fully embraced by everyone, nor would it be easily fulfilled. In the years following the end of hostilities, the subject of the war continued to permeate the national consciousness, as the subject of poetry, fiction, and numerous memoirs, as well as of documentaries and popular films. Its memory was enshrined in war memorials, first in Washington and then throughout the country. As journalist Neil Sheehan reported two decades after the end of the fighting, Vietnam had become "our national obsession."[11] With so much attention continuing to be devoted to the war, there inevitably emerged by the end of the decade renewed interest in recovering those who had been left behind.

Leading the charge for the recovery of MIAs was the National League of Families of American Prisoners and Missing in Southeast Asia, a small but highly effective lobby that first arose on the West Coast as a loosely organized movement and was formally incorporated in May 1970. Numbering only a few thousand members—all relatives of soldiers formally listed as MIA—the league was persistent, focused, and remarkably effective in raising public awareness of its agenda and ensuring that its issue became a national priority. By 1992, it had pressured governmental leaders into conducting at least 58 congressional hearings concerning the issue of Vietnam POWs and MIAs.[12] And though more than 15 years had passed since the end of the war, a 1991 *Wall Street Journal/ NBC News* poll showed that 69 percent of Americans continued to believe that their countrymen were being held against their will in Indochina, and over half believed that their government was doing too little to rescue them.[13] Not a single claim of living American MIAs in Southeast Asia had ever been verified, but continued distrust of the government's truthfulness on anything having to do with the Vietnam War overrode the lack of physical evidence. As Michael Allen argued in his book, *Until the Last Man Comes Home*, "MIA activists used the search for the missing to focus attention on their own victimization, fostering hostility toward Vietnam and distrust of their own government."[14] The league and other MIA activists were intent on holding accountable governmental leaders across the political spectrum—from Henry Kissinger, who represented "the political elites who sent Americans to war only to abandon them," to John Kerry, who represented "the anti-war activists alleged to have stabbed them in the back."[15]

With the passage of time and through ensuing presidential administrations, from Ford to Carter, and Reagan to George H. W. Bush, the issue of the MIAs only increased in visibility and political importance. Turning the page on Vietnam had proved to be impossible. During the final year of the Bush presidency, the administration formulated an official response with the creation of the Joint Task Force—Full Accounting (JTF-FA), a military-run operation whose mission was to "achieve the fullest possible accounting for Americans still unaccounted for as a result of the war in Indochina."[16] The JTF-FA was given substantial resources to field teams of specialists—archaeologists, anthropologists, ordinance experts, medical officers, photographers, mortuary specialists, translators and the like—to investigate reports, credible and otherwise, of Americans left behind in Indochina. With an annual budget in excess of $100 million, the cost of recovering the missing was estimated in 1992 at $1.7 million per remains.[17] Although the primary mission for the JTF-FA was Indochina, it also deployed teams elsewhere to identify claims and recover remains from World War II and Korea. To be sure, the work was not only expensive, it was risky. As Neil Sheehan reported in 1995, the recovery teams during the first years of the JTF-FA faced "three great perils," which made their fieldwork exceedingly dangerous: an abundance of poisonous snakes, unexploded ordnance often found at recovery sites, and the prevalence of malaria and other tropical diseases. Notwithstanding these challenges, the nation had once again committed substantial resources and personnel to Vietnam. As the *New York Times* observed in 2002, "There is no military mission more relentless than the United States' hunt for its missing soldiers in Indochina."[18]

OVER THE YEARS Michael O'Donnell's poems had offered consolation to fellow veterans, and his recognition as a war poet offered some measure of comfort to Patsy, Marcus, and Jane. Yet the inescapable fact remained that Mike was a missing person lost tragically to the war. Although his status had been changed to deceased in 1978, neither his family nor the US Army considered the matter closed. In the years following the delivery of the two telegrams in March 1970, the O'Donnells received regular communications from the Office of the Adjutant General, the army's department charged with keeping the families of MIAs informed both on recent developments related to their particular case and, more generally, to report on its ongoing work. It was the office's practice to send letters to MIA families about once a month, year after year. Prior to the creation of the JTF-FA in 1992, the O'Donnells had already accumulated a large box filled with correspondence and reports on possible sightings of the helicopter crash site, the discovery of artifacts or human remains, and even sightings of Michael himself—all of which proved to be false. Well intended though these letters were, the immediate effect on the family was to be reminded regularly of the excruciating circumstance of Michael's indeterminate state. Without physical evidence or further testimony from witnesses, there could be no real closure, but despite so much correspondence, the army simply had little to say. The creation of the JTF-FA would change all of this for the O'Donnells.

Within its first year of operations, the JTF-FA made investigating the loss of helicopter UH-1H 262 a priority, in large part because there existed reasonably accurate information about the location where O'Donnell and his crew had been shot down. In November 1993, a first attempt was made by air to locate the crash site in the "Dragon's Tail," an isolated and mountainous region at the northeast boundary of Ratanakiri Province. Although the after action reports described the general area where the helicopter had disappeared, the specific location of the wreckage deep in the jungle, approximately 86 kilometers northeast of Ban Lung, would be hard to pin down. In truth, conditions would make it nearly impossible. The dense jungle canopy and the deep ravine where the crash occurred would prevent sightings from the air, even at very low altitudes, and a ground search would be even more difficult. The recovery team knew that after nearly three decades in an extremely humid tropical environment, populated largely by vipers, pythons, cobras, the occasional tiger, and countless disease-bearing insects, the weathered helicopter would not be discovered easily and, if it was located at all, was likely not in good condition or even intact. It was possible the ship and all that it contained had been incinerated altogether; after all, Jim Lake and the other witnesses had reported that after being fired upon, the helicopter exploded and plunged to earth, disappearing beneath the jungle canopy as it was engulfed in flames. And if anything had survived the crash, it could have been taken by foragers who passed through the area over the years, collecting scrap metal and war remains that they could sell for cash. Finally, the team knew that whatever did remain at the site would have been swallowed by the dense jungle long ago, making the wreckage all but invisible. Finding anything at all would be like finding a needle in a haystack, but the recovery crew was experienced, resourceful, and prepared.

After determining that the site could not be located from the air or even from the ground without more specific geographic information, the recovery team decided to try another approach. They set off for Kontum to interview local Cambodian and Vietnamese villagers known to have been foragers, who knew the area around Ratanakiri Province and might have promising leads. Over the next two years, a series of interviews with villagers produced meaningful results, including the recovery of objects that had already been taken from the wreckage and the disclosure of more detailed information about the location of the crash site, even though these foragers readily acknowledged that they did not know whether the site was actually in Vietnam or in Cambodia. In January 1994, a Vietnamese villager offered for sale metal identification tags (dog tags) for Berman Ganoe and John Hoskin, two of O'Donnell's crewmates, which he claimed to have recovered himself from the site some years before. He reported that the helicopter was located in a muddy ravine and that the number 262 was still visible on the tail boom.

The following year another US recovery team visited Kontum to interview several Vietnamese foragers who corroborated the earlier testimony and offered additional artifacts and human remains that they had taken from the site. One of the objects in their possession—which was particularly puzzling—was an identification tag with the name "O'DDONNELL MICHEAL D." Although O'Donnell's name was misspelled, the tag was otherwise correct, including blood type and serial number. Since GIs sometimes replaced lost dog tags locally, errors of this kind were not infrequent, making it possible that the object had actually been found in the wreckage. The Vietnamese men also provided detailed information about how to reach the site where they claimed to have found the artifacts. A few months later, using that information, the recovery team found an area containing wreckage but determined that it was not the actual crash site; rather, it was an area where some of the wreckage had been moved to be cut for scrap. They were making progress—the artifacts and wreckage were determined to be associated with helicopter UH-1H 262—but the crash site, although presumably close by, remained elusive.

Finally, in March 1997, the villagers agreed to lead a joint team of Vietnamese and Cambodian officials on an expedition to find the site. Led by Thao Lao, an 80-year-old forager, who claimed to have been there before, the group departed from Cambodian border "Post 18," and for the next five days, journeying by foot and on a bamboo raft, made their way to an old helicopter landing zone known to be in the vicinity of the crash site. From there the team was directed to the west through the jungle and, at last, found the wreckage they had sought for so long. "The area is at the base of a mountain in a spring-fed creek that is located at the base of a deep V-shaped ravine (approximately 30 to 45 degree slopes

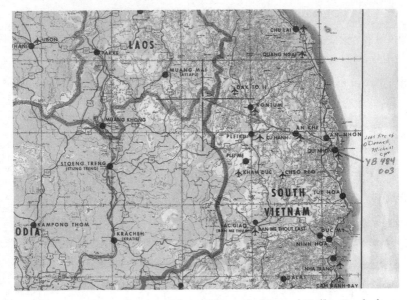

Military map showing location of the crash site in the "Dragon's Tail" in Cambodia.
PHOTO PROVIDED BY US ARMY.

on both sides)," the expedition leaders reported. "The creek flows in a southwest to northeasterly direction. The surrounding project area has very dense bamboo and secondary growth vegetation. The nearest village, Ta Veng, is approximately 40 kilometers to the southwest of the site. There are no major roads or trails to the site."[19] The wreckage, they said, was "surrounded by a heavy bamboo thicket," making it all but invisible even at close range.

After nearly three decades, Michael O'Donnell's helicopter had finally been found. Now it remained for the group to find what else was there and, to the extent they could, to determine what had happened to the crew. The team was pleased to see that the site was largely intact and contained a large amount of wreckage spread over a 20-by-30-meter area bisected by a small stream, which the team called "No Name Creek" (identified on the map as the Yak Yin Stream). The ruined helicopter, with tail number 262 clearly evident, was broken into several large pieces, running east to west across the stream. The reconnaissance team fully documented all that they found but otherwise did not disturb the site. They also reported on the suitability of the area for the kind of large-scale excavation required to do justice to a site of this size and complexity. Although the site was exceptionally remote and logistically difficult to access, the team had seen a great deal of evidence and therefore recommended that the site be excavated.

Tail boom of helicopter 262 at the crash site.
PHOTO FROM REPORT CILHI 1995-028.

The JTF-FA quickly agreed, and soon began planning the recovery effort, which they scheduled to take place during the dry season the following year—in January and February of 1998. The recovery team would consist of eight Americans, led by Dr. C. E. "Hoss" Moore, a highly experienced forensic anthropologist from Kansas who had not served in Vietnam because of a hearing defect, but who was committed to "do his bit" to help close the final chapter on the war.[20] In 24 years of service to the Defense Prisoner of War/Missing in Action Accounting Agency (DPAA), Moore led 86 overseas deployments, searching for lost service members from Vietnam and Korea, as well as from the World War II era. In addition to Moore, the full team would include a medic, an explosive ordnance disposal technician, a linguist, a mortuary affairs specialist, a photographer, an army captain to serve as team commander, and a staff sergeant who would be the noncommissioned officer-in-charge. In addition to the Americans, the group was to be accompanied by 2 Cambodian military officers and 80 Cambodian civilians who had been hired in Ban Lung.

On January 12, 1998, an advance group was transported on two French-made AS-350 helicopters for the one-hour flight from Ban Lung to an improvised landing zone near the crash site. Upon arrival, the team first set out to enlarge the landing zone to accommodate the larger helicopters that would bring in the rest of the group. Next, they built an equipment storage facility and set up the campsite where the team expected to remain for about four weeks. Once the entire team was in place and relatively settled, the recovery process began in earnest. The first step was to conduct a "pedestrian surface search 200 meters up and downstream of the aircraft wreckage and 50 meters up each slope of the ravine." The survey yielded significant findings, including especially, as Moore reported, "a complete helicopter in an active streambed." All the findings were marked with flags, including visible aircraft wreckage, material evidence related to the presence of air crew and passengers, and other life-support equipment. In only a short time they had found more than 100 objects, but finding human remains, if they were to be found at all, would require closer examination and systematic excavation of the area. This was always the most difficult part of any recovery effort. As Caroline Alexander reported on the recovery work of a different team excavating in Vietnam, "the task at hand seemed preposterous and futile, belonging more to the realm of myth than to reality. A man had been leached into the earth, and the earth was now being turned inside out to find him."[21] Yet, this was exactly the task at hand for Moore and his crew. As Moore observed, "I have excavated sites in many different types of terrain: swamps, mountains, rice paddies, flat ground, triple canopy jungles, and the challenges are endless." The work to recover the remains of O'Donnell and his crew would be painstaking and meticulous.

The next step was to establish archaeological grids for excavation, which required that the entire area be cleared of all bamboo and secondary growth vegetation except trees greater than 10 centimeters in diameter. The precinct to be excavated was then divided into 41 grids, each measuring 5 by 5 meters, meaning that an area of more than 1,000 square meters would have to be "turned inside out." Then, they needed to redirect the flow of the stream away from the grids and, in so doing, create a dam that would provide a reservoir for wet-screening the soil that would be removed from the creek bed. Elsewhere on the site, the team constructed two additional dry-screening areas. When the remaining site preparation work was finished, the team would construct three additional dams to impede the flow of water through the rest of the area, allowing the workers access to use their picks, shovels, and trowels to remove the soil, grid by grid. Based on the particular site conditions within each grid, Moore would determine how deeply the teams were to dig. Normally this would vary from about 10 centimeters for the dry areas to 60 centimeters for the creek-bed areas. They then set to work, and for the next several weeks conducted a full excavation of the site.

Michael O'Donnell's helicopter at crash site with
flags marking found materials.
PHOTO FROM REPORT CILHI 1995-028.

Workers clearing the crash site of all vegetation.
PHOTO FROM REPORT CILHI 1995-028.

Under exceptionally difficult circumstances—including unfriendly encounters with a six-foot-long black cobra, several bamboo pit vipers, and a twenty-five-foot-long black python, the presence of unexploded ordnance, and the ongoing challenge of a stream flowing through the middle of the excavation area—the team was able to recover a significant amount of material from the earth, the most important of which consisted of 40 bone fragments and 19 teeth. For a recovery effort of this kind, such an outcome was extraordinarily positive. Another recovery effort in Vietnam involving approximately 4,500 hours of excavation had yielded only a single tooth.[22] With any luck, these findings would allow for the identification of several members of the doomed mission, but there was no guarantee.

Having accomplished their mission, Moore and his team cleared the site on February 9, bringing with them not only the human remains and personal effects they had recovered but also the tail boom with the ship number 262 stenciled in large yellow characters. The work ahead would also be long and difficult. This included identification of the remains, documentation of all materials, and the return of the missing to their families for burial—all of which was to be done by the Central Identification Laboratory, Hawaii (CILHI), located at Hickam Air Force Base in Honolulu. Containing the largest forensic laboratory in the world, the CILHI analyzed materials found by recovery teams working throughout the world. The work relied primarily on the

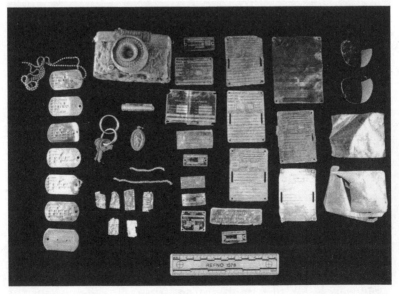

Photo of personal objects recovered at the crash site.
PHOTO FROM REPORT CILHI 1995-028.

examination of dental records and analysis of DNA to determine the identities of the missing.

Shortly after the team had concluded their fieldwork in the winter of 1998, Patsy was notified that they had found Michael's helicopter and had recovered human remains, which they believed were from the crew and passengers. For the DNA analysis to proceed, the scientists at CILHI needed to collect DNA samples from living relatives of the soldiers who had perished. Patsy provided the requested material and was told that there would be a long process ahead, perhaps several years in duration. After so many years, Patsy was accustomed to waiting when it came to her brother. She remembers writing to Marcus at the time, "I guess I'm grateful that the country bothered to go find him and bring him home. The Army was always aware of the location of the crash site and carried all these men as 'missing' all of these years because they were spies. I guess they finally 'feel safe to call the war insane.'" For Patsy, the government's reluctance to find her brother had always been about the secrecy of his mission and their unwillingness to accept responsibility for deaths occurring outside of the authorized war zone. After informing Marcus, Jane, and others about the discovery in Cambodia, Patsy settled in to wait.

The CILHI team had a significant amount of material to analyze, and it was their practice to complete all the work of examining dental records, DNA, and other materials before contacting any of the families with the final results. In May of 2001, more than three years after the completion of the fieldwork in Cambodia, Patsy received word from the Army Office of Repatriation and Family Affairs. "A casualty officer and a 'mortuary affairs' man came to our home," she reported to Marcus. "I was given a black spiral-bound book from the Army's Central Identification Laboratory in Hawaii, detailing the recovery of Mike's remains, along with those of the six other Americans and five unknown Montagnard personnel aboard the aircraft that day." The officers told Patsy that the remains would soon be returned for burial.

The spiral-bound book sent to each family was a detailed report outlining the excavation work that was conducted in Cambodia and the subsequent scientific analysis that led to CILHI's conclusions. In addition to identifying the remains of several (but not all) of the Americans who had been on board the helicopter, the report concluded that the perimortem trauma evident in the skeletal remains indicated that the men most likely died at the time of the crash. After so many years of anguish and disappointment, the news was bittersweet. Patsy and Marcus reflected on all that had happened. Both had recognized long ago that Michael had died in Cambodia, and in the intervening years they had gotten on with their lives. Patsy was sorry that her parents never had the chance to know what had happened to their son, and especially that his death had been quick with little evidence of suffering. But for Marcus, the finality of the news was hard to accept: "When I heard that the crash site had been found I finally gave in to my years-long feeling that Michael was not coming home." He further added:

> I was devastated at the thought that he and the others had been there at the crash site in the jungle, in Cambodia for all those years. I tried to imagine the solitude, the aloneness, and

the terrible beauty of the jungle slowly reclaiming and obliter-
ating their remains. I cried, I leaned hard on poor Charlotte, I
wrote poems and songs imagining the day he was shot down,
what the war was like for him, how death came and took him,
and how he was finally found.

Along with the report, the army also sent to Patsy a small
package containing a second metal dog tag; this one with Mike's
first name misspelled. Badly weathered, the tag and neck chain
had been excavated from the same grid where they had found her
brother's remains.

Michael O'Donnell's dog tag excavated at the crash site beside
his remains. Note the misspelling of his first name.

PHOTO FROM REPORT CILHI 1995-028.

Chapter 8

RECONCILIATION

I feel the spring far off, far off,
    The faint, far scent of bud and leaf—
Oh, how can spring take heart to come
    To a world in grief,
    Deep grief?

The sun turns north, the days grow long,
    Later the evening star grows bright—
How can the daylight linger on
    For men to fight,
    Still fight?

The grass is waking in the ground,
    Soon it will rise and blow in waves—
How can it have the heart to sway
    Over the graves,
    New graves?

Under the boughs where lovers walked
    The apple-blooms will shed their breath—
But what of all the lovers now
    Parted by Death
    Grey Death?

—SARA TEASDALE,
"Spring in War-Time," 1917

The war in Vietnam has been over for more than a generation, and soon we will mark the 50th anniversary of Michael O'Donnell's death in Cambodia. During the intervening years, the soldiers, politicians, diplomats, generals, activists, and others who defined that era have aged, and many have since left the scene. In that time the trauma of Vietnam has receded as an urgent national issue, but it has emerged as a defining event in our history. Moreover, as recent military adventures in Iraq, Afghanistan, and elsewhere make clear, we have not learned all that we might from this tragic period in our history. The war in the Persian Gulf, which was initiated in 1990 with clear objectives and public support, was resolved decisively a little more than six months later. By contrast, the war in Iraq, which was started under false pretenses in 2003 by a deceptive administration, ended with devastating long-term consequences, and along the way divided the nation. What, then, has Vietnam taught us, and what have we failed to learn? Can there be reconciliation over Vietnam for the soldiers who were there, their families, or the nation? What even does it mean to become reconciled in the context of such a tragedy? These questions have no easy answers, but I believe there remains more to be learned by asking them, and by trying to understand with the benefit of time and reflection what happened to our nation in the aftermath of this tragic era. As the Greek soldier and playwright Aeschylus wrote, "He who learns must suffer. And even in our sleep, pain that cannot forget, falls drop by drop upon the heart, and in our own despair, against our will, comes wisdom to us by the awful grace of God."[1] What wisdom have we acquired from this insane war?

To begin, if we are to judge from the abundant written record—including so many revelations from those who were involved—most would agree that the war itself failed to accomplish the objectives that were presented to justify it in the first place. The war did not prevent the spread of communism in Southeast Asia, and it surely did not destroy or in any way diminish the Communist leaders who prosecuted the war, especially Ho Chi Minh, the charismatic leader for whom a reunited Vietnam's most populous city is now named. In time, and well after the war, we all learned that communism as a political and economic idea was actually doomed from the start. Nowhere in the world has the communist experiment actually succeeded or endured in anything like the form that inspired the movement in the first place. But most important, what mattered to Ho and his followers—and should have mattered to us—was the conviction that a nation has the right to self-determination. That, after all, was what the fight was really about, and what drove an under-resourced but determined people to sacrifice so much and ultimately to prevail, just as the American colonists had against the British so long ago. If the American leaders did not understand this, the Vietminh soldiers doing the fighting certainly did. As Duc Thanh, a North Vietnamese soldier-poet wrote in July 1966:

> Tonight the wind is cold on bamboo trees.
> The moon hides behind the mountain's top.
> In sadness the river ripples.
>
> You do not understand the way of truth.
> Life must be spent for the people's good.

I picked a violet to tuck into my book.
Tears mixed with the violet's ink
To weave into my writing.
All the wishes I send, so you will understand.

I cannot return
While the enemy is in Vietnam.
I must fight until our country is unified.
All people in the North and South
Will welcome the day when we can meet again.[2]

For those who genuinely bothered to understand Ho Chi Minh and followed the arc of his life, this core principle was never in doubt, and he himself never said otherwise. Communism was the vehicle but never the goal. Our leaders did not understand this because they were preoccupied with a different question: the risk posed by the global expansion of communism on the American way of life. With the benefit of hindsight, it is remarkable, and highly instructive, that the "best and the brightest" simply did not figure this out sooner.

With a more complete understanding of events and their impact over time, most Americans have become reconciled to the idea that the war was a strategic and political failure. For the most part we have reconciled our differences with the Vietnamese people, whom we now embrace as strong trading partners and friends. But it is certainly harder to speak of reconciliation when we consider the deceitful and immoral actions taken by our own leaders who willingly and knowingly sent American citizens to their destruction to advance a strategy that they knew would fail. As Larry Heinemann said, in this sense the war was a "shuck."[3]

Government leaders sacrificed their own people simply to post-
pone acknowledging that they had been wrong. As Shakespeare
wrote in *Henry V*:

> But if the cause not be good,
> the king himself hath a heavy reckoning to make ...
>
> Now, if these men do not die well,
> it will be a black matter for the king that led them to it.[4]

Although a great deal has been written on the tragic era of
Vietnam, ultimately what we must confront is not a complicated political question; it is a simple, moral one. There cannot
and should not be any reconciliation with such mendacity and
moral bankruptcy. That is why character is the most important
quality required of leaders—more important even than the
quality of intellect embodied by the celebrated team profiled in
The Best and the Brightest. Ralph Waldo Emerson observed that
character was an ineffable quality, "a reserved force which acts
directly by presence, and without means."[5] For Emerson, character is something deeper and more enduring than just the accumulation of actions. He wrote, for example, on the character
of George Washington, "We cannot find the smallest part of the
personal weight of Washington, in the narrative of his exploits."[6]
If the leaders in the era of Vietnam had demonstrated a greater
capacity to wield their power with humility, to learn from those
who were knowledgeable rather than to manipulate and exploit
them, to base their decision-making on principles of integrity
and truthfulness rather than expediency and self-interest, and
to act with courage in doing what they knew to be right, the

outcome in Vietnam would almost certainly have been very different. Emerson observed that leaders of character ultimately serve as the conscience of the society to which they belong. The failures of Vietnam, and the horrific loss of life that was a consequence, surely reflect what was missing from our leaders in that time.

In his penetrating study of the origins of the conflict of Vietnam, H. R. McMaster argued that the path to war was neither an inevitable consequence of the Cold War nor was it fundamentally about containing communism.[7] Rather, McMaster argued that from November 1963 through May 1965, President Johnson and his civilian advisers deepened the American commitment in Vietnam through a series of near-term political decisions that were focused on advancing their domestic agenda, and not on a careful and informed understanding of the issues in Vietnam. By virtue of a leadership style that was both insecure and consensus driven, the president deliberately excluded from his deliberations the opinions of those who might disagree with him, including especially the Joint Chiefs of Staff and other military leaders. As a result of inexperience and arrogance, Johnson and his team of civilians, however intelligent and rational they might have been, simply did not appreciate that "human sacrifices in war evoke strong emotions, creating a dynamic that defies systems analysis quantification."[8] Once committed to war and seeing no easy way out, they gradually increased American involvement without disclosing either the facts or many of their own actions to the public. To make matters worse, the record is clear that as early as May 1964, months before he began to escalate the war with the Gulf of Tonkin Resolution, Johnson was fully aware of the implications of his actions to increase US involvement, as he observed to McGeorge Bundy, "It's damn easy to get into a war, but . . . it's going to be harder to ever extricate yourself if you get in." He also acknowledged the likelihood of failure: "[L]ooks to me that we are getting into another Korea. . . . I don't see what we can ever hope to get out of this."[9] At the time of this conversation, the United States had lost only 400 soldiers in Vietnam.

Over the next three years, as the president continued to escalate the war in Vietnam, and the human costs and strategic failures became increasingly visible to the public, the goal shifted from securing a free and independent South Vietnam to maintaining American credibility. The war was lost even before it had begun because the administration's futile desire for a "limited war" simply could not be reconciled with what the military leaders believed would be necessary to actually win. As McMaster concluded:

> The disaster in Vietnam was not the result of impersonal forces but a uniquely human failure, the responsibility for which was shared by President Johnson and his principal military and civilian advisors. The failings were many and reinforcing: arrogance, weakness, lying in pursuit of self-interest, and, above all, the abdication of responsibility to the American people.[10]

IF THE WAR was lost before it started because of failure of leadership, it was ended because the weight of public opposition ultimately prevailed. Those elected officials, like Senators J. William

Fulbright and Eugene McCarthy, who were committed to ending the war; veterans returning from the war such as Ron Kovic, Philip Caputo, and W. D. Ehrhart who spoke honestly about their experiences; activists who harnessed public opposition to political action; and especially the voice of a free press all contributed to exposing the truth about the slowly unfolding tragedy in Vietnam. In time, the American people rose powerfully to oppose the policies of their government at levels unprecedented in the nation's history. In that time, it was the noisy voice of a functioning democracy that prevailed in holding elected officials accountable and forcing the United States to exit the war.

If the war in Vietnam resembled the Civil War for the ways it divided the nation, one major difference between these conflicts can be found in the ways government leaders understood their obligations to those they sacrificed on the battlefield. In contrast to the leaders in the era of Vietnam who committed a moral obscenity in sending soldiers to fight a war under false pretenses and with no chance of success, President Lincoln well understood the human consequences of his war. In myriad accounts of his leadership throughout the conflict, and in his own words, it is clear that Lincoln appreciated the heavy burden of their sacrifice, saying at Gettysburg, "[F]rom these honored dead we take increased devotion to that cause for which they gave the last full measure of devotion—that we here highly resolve that these dead shall not have died in vain." The ultimate test for Lincoln was whether the principles that had ignited the war (preservation of the Union) and then later sustained it (emancipation) were worth the cost in human lives. He faced that excruciating question every day of the war, carrying it with grace and resolve until Robert E. Lee's surrender at Appomattox.

In both of these wars the American people were able to witness the brutality and loss in new and unprecedented ways; in the 1860s through the advent of photography, which documented the unfolding carnage in real time and made it available to all; and a century later through the advent of television news, which each day brought live images of the fighting, the suffering, and the dead into homes across the country and around the world. In both of these wars, the real cost and tragic consequences were lost on no one.

In the aftermath of Vietnam, the movement to commemorate the war deviated from earlier traditions in its emphasis by the veterans themselves on recognizing those who died rather than the cause or its leaders. For the first time in American history, those who had done the fighting, for the most part did not support the cause or respect their leaders. Moreover, because the war had been the source of so much national conflict and because the cause had been futile, the returning veterans had no victory to celebrate and no public to welcome them. As W. D. Ehrhart wrote on the occasion of his return from the war in 1967:

San Francisco airport—

no more corpsmen stuffing ruptured chests
with cotton balls and not enough heat tabs
to eat a decent meal.

I asked some girl to sit
and have a Coke with me.

She thought I was crazy;
I thought she was going to call a cop.

I bought a ticket for Philadelphia.
At the loading gate, they told me:
"Thank you for flying TWA;
we hope you will enjoy your flight."

No brass bands;
no flags,
no girls,
no cameramen.

Only a small boy who asked me
what the ribbons on my jacket meant.[11]

In the years that followed the US withdrawal, the American people eventually recognized that Vietnam veterans had been done an injustice, but even today, after all this time, not enough has been done to correct past mistakes. While the nation had finally begun, through ceremony and memorial, to honor the soldiers who died in Vietnam, it did not match that commitment with substantive investment in the well-being of those who survived.[12] If one measure of a nation is how it treats those whose service it no longer needs, and those who have little power or influence, the treatment of our veterans provides an important opportunity for careful reassessment. By war's end, the Vietnam veterans had already given "the full measure of their devotion," and in so doing had exhausted their military value to the government. Many of them needed support in dealing with devastating disabilities, illness, and other lingering effects of post-traumatic stress disorder. But while the military continued to secure the funds needed to invest in the latest weapons systems, to operate successfully a highly complex military-industrial complex, and to recruit young soldiers for new wars, it has decidedly not met its obligation to those left behind by earlier wars who required the medical care and other benefits they were promised.[13] This disparity between words and deeds is a manifestation of the political priorities and values of our leaders. Despite the price they paid for the nation, neither the veterans of Vietnam nor those of later wars have received the full measure of support necessary to rebuild healthy and rewarding lives. This too is a moral issue that people of conscience must address.

SHORTLY AFTER I began work on this project, I reached out to Marcus Sullivan, who had recently retired from a long career as a high school English teacher in Illinois. When I first interviewed him, Marcus was living in Milwaukee and providing full-time care for his wife, Charlotte, who was then suffering from the debilitating impact of type 1 diabetes. He expressed full support for this project and pledged to help in every way possible. Marcus had great admiration for his friend and believed that his story was important, both on its own terms and for what it revealed about a difficult period in America. In a very short time, he became an essential partner in conducting research and interviews for this book, and, along the way, we became good friends. In the early phases of our work together, Marcus and I were able to locate and then interview several of the people closest to the story. Our first visit was to Las Vegas to meet with Patsy.

For most of her adult life, Patsy McNevin has carried the family burden for dealing with the loss of her brother. She spent three decades asking members of the military and government, elected officials, and others to do what they could to help locate her brother and enable her family to experience some kind of resolution. For nearly 50 years she has overseen Michael's literary legacy, making sure that his poetry has been used in ways consistent with his intentions and respectful of the circumstances in which it was written. For the most part, she has done this work alone. As Marcus reflected on all that happened, he wrote, "It struck me how incredible Patsy was through the early days of all of this and also the frustration and anger she began to feel as well as the sadness as the years passed by with little or no word about Michael. Over the many years Patsy sent me anything and everything she got or found about Michael." Along the way, Patsy also did what she could to comfort her devastated parents, a task that was nearly impossible under the circumstances. The years had been hard for her, especially as the war receded into history, she lost her parents, and everyone else wanted to move on.

When Patsy met with us on that first visit, she was fully supportive of the project, offering to share with us a substantial archive of materials that she had accumulated, including military records and reports, correspondence, poems, photos, and clippings. Beyond her support for the book project, it soon became clear to me that Patsy was also relieved finally to have others interested in telling her brother's story and carrying his legacy. With this book, Patsy thought that I could assume some of the responsibility that she, along with Marcus, had carried for so long. Over the years, I have visited Patsy several times, and throughout she has been helpful, supportive, and encouraging. Notwithstanding the passage of time, Patsy acknowledged that the loss is still difficult. "It doesn't seem to matter how many years have passed," she said. "I remain heartbroken." Now widowed after a long and happy marriage, Patsy is content that she did what she could for her brother, and she is gratified that his poetry continues to matter. On one of my visits to her home I noticed that her key chain, which was resting on the kitchen counter, had Mike's old, weathered dog tag attached to the ring. As she told me then, it made her feel a little better to have this small remembrance of her brother by her side each day. After Bette passed away in 2003, Patsy decided to place Mike's dog tag with her mother's remains and bury them together.

Jane, after spending a year in Brazil, returned home in 1971 to begin exploring a new future, but as she said, she felt truly lost. She traveled around the United States, returned to Tallahassee, and was married for a time before deciding to attend law school, which she found to be interesting and rewarding. Subsequently Jane remarried and embarked on a long and successful career in Florida state government. Recently retired, Jane and her husband Kris have lived on the Gulf Coast of Florida for more than 20 years. On my recent visit to their home, Jane reflected on her time with Mike as among the happiest of her life. To have lost someone she loved so deeply at such an early age was both tragic

*Jane in September
1969, the last time
she was with Mike.*
FAMILY PHOTO.

*Jane in 2005, at the
time I first met her.*
AUTHOR'S PHOTO.

and life-changing. Jane feels that with the benefit of time and experience, the hard edges of grief have softened, leaving her with warm memories and great sadness about a time when so much went wrong. Over the years, as I have worked on this book, Jane and Kris have also become dear friends.

For Marcus, losing his best friend and musical partner was a terrible blow. After returning from Vietnam, where he served as a combat engineer, Marcus built his life with Charlotte until she passed away in 2008, after a long illness. In recent years Marcus has remarried and lives happily in Madison, Wisconsin, with his wife, Cindy. He remains active in the local music scene and enjoys spending time with his and Cindy's grandchildren. Over the years Marcus has done much to keep the memory of his friend alive. In his work as a teacher, Marcus spoke frequently with his students about folk music, poetry, the Vietnam War, and especially Michael. On special occasions, he would even play for them some of the songs the duet had performed long ago in Whitewater and Old Town. In 1985, for a story on Michael for their evening news show, NBC News interviewed Marcus and filmed him performing some of their old songs in class. Although so much time had passed, Marcus still felt strange singing those songs without his friend by his side.

Marcus greatly regrets that he was unable to attend Michael's funeral at Arlington. As Patsy explained to him at the time, the army would not provide an exact date so they had very short notice to make the trip. When the date was finally provided in August 2001, Patsy offered to fly Marcus and Charlotte to Washington so that they could be there, but Charlotte was not well and could not travel, so Marcus was unable to get away.

A few years ago, I accompanied Marcus to Arlington National Cemetery for his first visit to Michael's grave site. As we entered Section 60, I observed that Michael's grave was no longer surrounded by open lawns awaiting the dead of future wars. That area today is crowded with gravestones, row upon row meticulously aligned, memorializing those killed in the cities and towns of Afghanistan and Iraq. As of this writing, the protracted conflict in the Middle East has cost more than 7,000 American lives and countless others, including those of civilians. Like the war in Vietnam, the wars in Iraq and Afghanistan have engendered much controversy. Yet, no longer do American citizens place the blame for controversial or misguided policies on the soldiers who

Marcus at Arlington National Cemetery, standing before Mike's grave.
AUTHOR'S PHOTO.

Section 60 at Arlington National Cemetery, autumn 2018.

PHOTO BY BRUCE DALE.

do the fighting and dying. In the decades since the end of the conflict in Vietnam, the nation has learned to distinguish between its civic responsibilities to question the government and its moral commitment to embrace those who served.

As we approached Michael's grave, Marcus said:

I loved Michael and I miss him every day. I miss what might have been for us if he had returned from Vietnam. I take solace in the memories of the two of us before the war when we were just college kids who became friends, found music and books and poetry together. After all these years, I think he would have been pleased. More than anything, Michael wanted to have an impact. We all knew that he would, but we thought that it would be with his music, not the war. But so it is that things turned out the way they did. O'Donnell would have loved all the attention and he would have been glad to know that his life mattered. We have that, and our memories. We go on.

As we were leaving Section 60, we passed a young woman seated on a blanket with a small child. They were quietly having a picnic in front of a white headstone, one amid a long row of headstones. We couldn't read the words inscribed on the face of the headstone, and we didn't want to intrude, but we couldn't help noticing that the grass beneath them was new.

ACKNOWLEDGMENTS

It is a pleasure to thank the many friends and colleagues who have supported my work on this project over the years. For help with matters large and small, I am grateful to Barbara Bridgers, Marie Enea, Sara Engoron, Jim Krivoski, Heather Lamb, Jeanette O'Keefe, John O'Keefe, Pat Piraino, Bob Tyrer, and Joan Wankmiller. For assistance with research, I extend my thanks to Ilya Bourtman and Teddy Weiss, and most recently Emily Hawk, who has been especially helpful in exploring the world of politics and culture in the 1960s, and in thinking through many of the ideas that are presented within these pages.

In the course of my research and writing I have had the privilege of meeting many of Michael O'Donnell's friends, both from his time in the army and from the years before. It is clear that Mike was beloved and admired by all who knew him. For their support and help in various ways, I am grateful to David Bushman, George Crawford, Frank Greco, Bobby Ross, Greg Stageburg, Don Summers, and Bill Watson. Roger Weaver, a seasoned helicopter pilot himself, generously shared with me his extensive knowledge, which included taking me on board a Vietnam-era

Huey so that I could understand just a little better what was involved for pilots who had to fly them in the middle of a war. Jim Lake has been unfailingly generous in answering questions and helping me to understand more about the world of helicopter pilots flying missions in the Central Highlands of Vietnam at the time he and O'Donnell were there. Dr. C. E. Moore, who led the excavation team in Cambodia, was most gracious in answering my questions and providing me with a better sense of all that was involved in the arduous and demanding work of recovering the missing.

I also had the pleasure of getting to know some of the most accomplished war poets of the Vietnam era, including especially Bill Ehrhart and John Balaban. My friend Bruce Dale has taken a lively interest in this project, including accompanying me on a visit to Arlington National Cemetery, where he made beautiful images for this book. Karen Gantz, my indefatigable agent, has supported this project in every way imaginable, and she introduced me to the remarkable Peter Osnos, whose support at PublicAffairs and throughout this project has made this book possible. At PublicAffairs, I am also grateful to Clive Priddle, Pete Garceau, Brynn Warriner, and Athena Bryan. Lisa Kaufman edited the manuscript with exemplary care and professionalism.

Many friends and family members have supported this project from the beginning. I am especially grateful to Jeff Thoke and Bill Reynolds, who read drafts of this book and offered helpful suggestions and advice. My sons, Teddy and Joel, have been a constant source of support on this book project and everything else. My wife, Sandra, has made it all possible. My dog, Allie, watched me write every word in this book and never complained.

Finally, without the support, generosity, and friendship of Patsy McNevin, Jane Mathis, and especially Marcus Sullivan, this book would never have been written. They have shared their knowledge and love of Michael, they have provided me with all kinds of assistance, and along the way they have become dear friends. It is to them and Sandra that this book is dedicated.

DANIEL H. WEISS
New York, March 2019

NOTES

Preface: Arlington

1. Excerpted from the full poem, reprinted in J. D. McClatchy, *Poets of the Civil War* (New York: The Library of America, 2005), 133–134.

2. For a comprehensive history of Arlington National Cemetery, see Robert M. Poole, *On Hallowed Ground: The Story of Arlington National Cemetery* (New York and London: Bloomsbury, 2009).

3. Poole, *On Hallowed Ground*, 12.

4. Poole, *On Hallowed Ground*, 14.

5. Poole, *On Hallowed Ground*, 13.

6. Poole, *On Hallowed Ground*, 13.

7. Poole, *On Hallowed Ground*, 10.

8. See Doris Kerns Goodwin, *Team of Rivals: The Political Genius of Abraham Lincoln* (New York: Simon & Schuster, 2005), 349–350.

9. Poole, *On Hallowed Ground*, 24.

10. Poole, *On Hallowed Ground*, 62.

11. Poole, *On Hallowed Ground*, 59–60.

12. See Drew Gilpin Faust, *This Republic of Suffering: Death and the American Civil War* (New York: Vintage, 2008), 212.

13. James F. Russling, "National Cemeteries," *Harper's New Monthly Magazine* 33 (August 1866), 322. Quoted in Faust, *This Republic of Suffering*, 233.

14. Faust, *This Republic of Suffering*, 213.

15. Quoted in Poole, *On Hallowed Ground*, 78.

16. Poole, *On Hallowed Ground*, 90–93.

17. *Where Valor Rests: Arlington National Cemetery* (Washington, DC: National Geographic, 2007), 40.

18. Posted on Arlington National Cemetery website.

Chapter 1. An Ice Cream Season

1. C. P. Cavafy, *The Collected Poems* (Oxford, UK: Oxford University Press, 2008), 3.

2. David L. Anderson, *Trapped by Success: The Eisenhower Administration and Vietnam, 1953–1961* (New York: Columbia University Press, 1991), xi.

3. The Truman National Security Council, quoted in H. R. McMaster, *Dereliction of Duty: Lyndon Johnson, Robert McNamara, the Joint Chiefs of Staff, and the Lies That Led to Vietnam* (New York: HarperCollins, 2017), 34.

4. Arnold A. Offner, *Another Such Victory: President Truman and the Cold War, 1945–1953* (Stanford, CA: Stanford University Press, 2002), 347.

5. Offner, *Another Such Victory*, 340.

6. Anderson, *Trapped by Success*, 16.

7. Anderson, *Trapped by Success*, 151.

8. William R. Haycraft, *Unraveling Vietnam: How American Arms and Diplomacy Failed in Southeast Asia* (Jefferson, NC: McFarland & Company, 2005), 75.

9. Lawrence Freedman, *Kennedy's Wars: Berlin, Cuba, Laos, and Vietnam* (New York: Oxford University Press, 2000), 291.

10. Lloyd C. Gardner and Ted Gittinger, eds., *Vietnam: The Early Decisions* (Austin: University of Texas Press, 1997), 31.

11. William J. Rust, *Kennedy in Vietnam* (New York: Scribner, 1985), 32.

12. James G. Blight, Janet M. Lang, and David A. Welch, *Vietnam If Kennedy Had Lived: Virtual JFK* (Lanham, MD: Rowman & Littlefield Publishers, 2009), 233.

13. McMaster, *Dereliction of Duty*, 8.

14. Quoted in McMaster, *Dereliction of Duty*, 26.

15. Quoted in McMaster, *Dereliction of Duty*, 27.

16. Quoted in Haycraft, *Unraveling Vietnam*, 95.

17. Blight, Lang, and Welch, *Vietnam If Kennedy Had Lived*, 238.

18. Marc H. Selverstone, "It's a Date: Kennedy and the Timetable for a Vietnam Troop Withdrawal," *Diplomatic History* 34, no. 3 (June 2010): 485.

19. Walter LaFeber, *The Deadly Bet: LBJ, Vietnam, and the 1968 Election* (Lanham, MD: Rowman & Littlefield Publishers, 2005), 3.

20. David Kaiser, *American Tragedy: Kennedy, Johnson, and the Origins of the Vietnam War* (Cambridge, MA: Harvard University Press, 2000), 410.

21. Francis M. Bator, "No Good Choices: LBJ and the Vietnam/Great Society Connection," *Diplomatic History* 32, no. 3 (June 2008): 315.

22. Eric Alterman, *When Presidents Lie: A History of Official Deception and Its Consequences* (New York: Viking Penguin, 2004), 176.

23. Alterman, *When Presidents Lie*, 179.

24. David Stiles Shipley, "Sacrifice, Victimization, and Mismanagement of Issues: LBJ's Vietnam Crisis," *Public Relations Review* 18, no. 3 (Autumn 1992), 282.

25. Quoted in Gordon M. Goldstein, *Lessons in Disaster: McGeorge Bundy and the Path to War in Vietnam* (New York: Holt, 2008), 3.

26. Quoted in Bernard Fall, "Interview with Ho Chi Minh: July 1962, Master of the Red Jab," *Reporting Vietnam: American Journalism 1959–1975* (New York: The Library of America, 2000), 18.

27. Shipley, "Sacrifice, Victimization, and Mismanagement of Issues," 282–283.

28. Edwin E. Moise, *Tonkin Gulf and the Escalation of the Vietnam War* (Chapel Hill: The University of North Carolina Press, 1996), 35.

29. Moise, *Tonkin Gulf*, xi.

30. Haycraft, *Unraveling Vietnam*, 116.

31. Moise, *Tonkin Gulf*, 225.

32. LaFeber, *The Deadly Bet*, 167.

33. Goldstein, *Lessons in Disaster*, 18.

Chapter 2. A Soldier in the Spring

1. Philip Caputo, *A Rumor of War* (New York: Henry Holt and Company, 1977), 95.

2. For a brief biography on Westmoreland, see Phillip B. Davidson, *Vietnam at War: The History 1946–1975* (New York: Oxford University Press, 1988), 369–386.

3. Stanley Karnow, *Vietnam: A History* (New York: Penguin Books, 1984), 361.

4. Chris Bishop, *Bell UH-1 Huey "Slicks" 1962–75* (Oxford, UK: Osprey Publishing, 2003), 15.

5. Philip D. Chinnery, *Vietnam: The Helicopter War* (Annapolis, MD: Naval Institute Press, 1991), vii.

6. Lee Riley Powell, *J. William Fulbright and America's Lost Crusade: Fulbright's Opposition to the Vietnam War* (Little Rock, AR: Rose Publishing Company, 1984), 236.

7. Eugene Brown, *J. William Fulbright: Advice and Dissent* (Iowa City: University of Iowa Press, 1985), 74.

8. Powell, *J. William Fulbright and America's Lost Crusade*, 93.

9. William C. Berman, *William Fulbright and the Vietnam War: The Dissent of a Political Realist* (Kent, OH: Kent State University Press, 1988), 50.

10. Melvin Small, *Antiwarriors: The Vietnam War and the Battle for America's Hearts and Minds* (Wilmington, DE: Scholarly Resources, 2002), 3.

11. Van Gosse, *Rethinking the New Left: An Interpretive History* (New York: Palgrave MacMillan, 2005), 86.

12. Small, *Antiwarriors*, 3.

13. Quoted in Marvin E. Gettleman, Jane Franklin, Marilyn B. Young, and H. Bruce Franklin, *Vietnam and America: The Most Comprehensive Documented History of the Vietnam War* (New York: Grove Press, 1995), 275.

14. Van Gosse, *Rethinking the New Left*, 94.

15. Adam Garfinkle, *Telltale Hearts: The Origins and Impact of the Vietnam War Movement* (New York: St. Martin's Press, 1996), 102.

16. Small, *Antiwarriors*, 90.

17. Van Gosse, *Rethinking the New Left*, 95.

Chapter 3. Vietnam Winter

1. Reprinted in *Poems from Captured Documents*, ed. Thanh T. Nguyen and Bruce Weigl (Amherst: The University of Massachusetts Press, 1994), 23.

2. Frances Fitzgerald, *Fire in the Lake* (New York: Vintage Books, 1972), 506.

3. On the SOG in Vietnam, see Frank Greco, *Running Recon* (Boulder, CO: Paladin Press, 2004).

4. Greco, *Running Recon*, 66.

Chapter 4. The Mission

1. Excerpted from "The Dead Wingman," reprinted in Randall Jarrell, *The Complete Poems* (New York: Farrar, Straus and Giroux, n.d.), 157.

2. The following account of what transpired on March 24, 1970, is based on reports written by Jim Lake, who commanded the mission, and Donald Summers, who had served in the 170th and was the unit's unofficial archivist and historian. Additional information was derived from interviews and Board of Inquiry reports filed by other pilots and crew members who were involved in the events of the day. See also Jim Lake's account published in Philip D. Chinnery, *Life on the Line: Stories of Vietnam Air Combat* (New York: St. Martin's Press, 1988), 200–204.

Chapter 5. Left Behind

1. Reprinted in *From Both Sides Now: The Poetry of the Vietnam War and Its Aftermath*, ed. Phillip Mahony (New York: Scribner Poetry, 1998), 123.

2. *Sunday Express*, March 12, 1972.

3. Larry Heinemann, "Prologue: Vietnam After All These Years," in *The United States and Vietnam from War to Peace*, ed. Robert M. Slabey (Jefferson, NC, and London: McFarland & Company, 1996), 12.

4. Reported in C. R. Herring, Congressional Services Report, RL 33452.

Chapter 6. Aftermath

1. Fox Butterfield, "Who Was This Enemy? Writings by North Vietnamese Soldiers: 1973," in *Reporting Vietnam: American Journalism 1959–1975*, ed. Milton J. Bates, Lawrence Lichty, Paul Miles, Ronald H. Spector, and Marilyn Young (New York: The Library of America, 1998), 654.

2. Reprinted in *A Corner of a Foreign Field: The Illustrated Poetry of the First World War*, selected by Fiona Waters (Hertfordshire, UK: Transatlantic Press, 2007), 187.

3. Bruce O. Solheim, *The Vietnam War Era: A Personal Journey* (Lincoln and London: University of Nebraska Press, 2008), 4.

4. Christian G. Appy, *American Reckoning: The Vietnam War and Our National Identity* (New York: Penguin Books, 2015), xiv.

5. William Grieder, "America and Defeat," *Washington Post*, May 4, 1975, 33.

6. Marita Sturken, *Tangled Memories: The Vietnam War, the AIDs Epidemic, and the Politics of Remembering* (Berkeley: University of California Press, 1997), 6.

7. Garry Wills, "Forgetting Vietnam Forecloses Analysis," *Baltimore Sun*, May 19, 1975.

8. Marc Jason Gilbert, "Lost Warriors: Viet Nam Veterans Among the Homeless," in Slabey, *The United States and Vietnam from War to Peace*, 91–92.

9. Gilbert, "Lost Warriors," 92.

10. John Wheeler is quoted in Gilbert, "Lost Warriors," 92.

11. Philip Caputo, *A Rumor of War* (New York: Henry Holt and Company, 1977), 349.

12. Caputo, *A Rumor of War*, 350.

13. Larry Heinemann, *Paco's Story* (New York: Penguin Books, 1986); Michael Herr, *Dispatches* (New York: Alfred A. Knopf, 1977); Ron Kovic, *Born on the Fourth of July* (New York: McGraw Hill Book Company, 1976); Tim O'Brien, *Going After Cacciato* (New York: Delacorte Press, 1978).

14. Kovic, *Born on the Fourth of July*, 19.

15. W. D. Ehrhart, *In the Shadow of Vietnam: Essays, 1977–1991* (Jefferson, NC, and London: McFarland & Company, 1991), 83.

16. Ehrhart, *In the Shadow of Vietnam*, 97.

17. "Morning—A Death" was first published in the *New York Review of Books*, December 18, 1969. Reprinted with permission of Basil Paquet.

18. John Balaban, "In Celebration of Spring," from *Locusts at the Edge of Summer: New and Selected Poems*, c. 1997 by John Balaban. Reprinted with permission of the Permissions Company, on behalf of Copper Canyon Press, www.coppercanyon press.org.

19. Patrick Hagopian, *The Vietnam War in American Memory: Veterans, Memorials, and the Politics of Healing* (Amherst: University of Massachusetts Press, 2009), 96–97.

20. Hagopian, *The Vietnam War in American Memory*, 93.

21. Sturken, *Tangled Memories*, 12.

22. Kristin Ann Hass, *Carried to the Wall: American Memory and the Vietnam Veterans Memorial* (Berkeley: University of California Press, 1998), 14.

23. Personal correspondence with Patricia McNevin, 1986.

Chapter 7. Recovery

1. From *Thank You for Your Service: Collected Poems*, c. 2019 W. D. Ehrhart by permission of McFarland & Company, Box 611, Jefferson, NC, 28640, www.mcfarlandbooks.com.

2. Michael Sledge, *Soldier Dead: How We Recover, Identify, Bury, and Honor Our Military Fallen* (New York, Columbia University Press, 2005), 32.

3. Quoted in Sledge, *Soldier Dead*, 34.

4. Drew Gilpin Faust, *This Republic of Suffering: Death and the American Civil War* (New York: Vintage, 2008), 217–218.

5. Faust, *This Republic of Suffering*, 229.

6. Quoted in Faust, *This Republic of Suffering*, 229–230.

7. Faust, *This Republic of Suffering*, 217–219.

8. Sledge, *Soldier Dead*, 9–15.

9. Quoted in Michael J. Allen, *Until the Last Man Comes Home: POWs, MIAs, and the Unending Vietnam War* (Chapel Hill: The University of North Carolina Press, 2009), 137.

10. Allen, *Until the Last Man Comes Home*, 2.

11. Susan Sheehan, "The Last Battle," *New Yorker* (April 24, 1995), 78–87.

12. Referenced in Allen, *Until the Last Man Comes Home*, 308n5.

13. Allen, *Until the Last Man Comes Home*, 2.

14. Allen, *Until the Last Man Comes Home*, 10.

15. Allen, *Until the Last Man Comes Home*, 5.

16. Sheehan, "The Last Battle," 78.

17. Allen, *Until the Last Man Comes Home*, 285.

18. Cited in Allen, *Until the Last Man Comes Home*, 3.

19. Reported in document CILHI 1995-028.

20. Michael Hayes, "No Name Creek: Recovery of Remains 30 Years Later of RT Pennsylvania & Bikini Red Three" (Special Operations.Com /MACVSOG/), 2.

21. Caroline Alexander, "Across the River Styx: The Mission to Retrieve the Dead," *The New Yorker*, October 25, 2004, 50.

22. Alexander, "Across the River Styx," 48.

Chapter 8. Reconciliation

1. Quoted in Edith Hamilton, *The Greek Way* (New York: Norton, 1930), 61.

2. Thanh T. Nguyen and Bruce Weigl, ed., *Poems from Captured Documents* (Amherst: The University of Massachusetts Press, 1994), 28–29.

3. Larry Heinemann, "Prologue: Vietnam After All These Years," in *The United States and Vietnam from War to Peace*, ed. Robert M. Slabey (Jefferson, NC, and London: McFarland & Company, 1996), 12.

4. William Shakespeare, *Henry V*, act 4, scene 1. Quoted in Sledge, *Soldier Dead*, 27.

5. Ralph Waldo Emerson, "Character," *Complete Works*.

6. Emerson, "Character," *Complete Works*.

7. H. R. McMaster, *Dereliction of Duty, Lyndon Johnson, Robert McNamara, the Joint Chiefs of Staff, and the Lies That Led to Vietnam* (New York: Harper-Collins, 2017), 323–324.

8. McMaster, *Dereliction of Duty*, 327.

9. Quoted in McMaster, *Dereliction of Duty*, 325 and 416n3.

10. McMaster, *Dereliction of Duty*, 333–334.

11. From *Thank You for Your Service: Collected Poems*, c. 2019, W. D. Ehrhart by permission of McFarland & Company.

12. Marc Jason Gilbert, "Lost Warriors: Viet Nam Veterans Among the Homeless," in *The United States and Vietnam from War to Peace*, ed. Slabey, 91–112.

13. James Wright, *Enduring Vietnam: An American Generation and Its War* (New York: Thomas Dunne Books, 2017), 322–323.

INDEX

DANIEL WEISS is the President and CEO of the Metropolitan Museum of Art. He is a member of the Council on Foreign Relations, Vice Chair of the Samuel H. Kress Foundation, and is a member of the boards of the Yale School of Management, the Library of America, the Wallace Foundation, and the Posse Foundation. He was previously President of Haverford College, President of Lafayette College, Dean of the Krieger School of Arts & Sciences at Johns Hopkins University, Chair of the Johns Hopkins History of Art Department, and a consultant with Booz, Allen & Hamilton. The author or editor of six books and numerous articles, he has been supported by research grants from the National Endowment of the Humanities, the Andrew W. Mellon Foundation, Harvard University, and the Samuel H. Kress Foundation. Daniel Weiss is the recipient of the Van Courtlandt Elliott Prize from the Medieval Academy of America and the Centennial Medal from the Foreign Policy Association, and he is a member of the Society of Scholars at Johns Hopkins University. He lives in New York City.

To read Michael O'Donnell's poetry and hear his music, go to www.InThatTime.com.

PublicAffairs is a publishing house founded in 1997. It is a tribute to the standards, values, and flair of three persons who have served as mentors to countless reporters, writers, editors, and book people of all kinds, including me.

I. F. STONE, proprietor of *I. F. Stone's Weekly*, combined a commitment to the First Amendment with entrepreneurial zeal and reporting skill and became one of the great independent journalists in American history. At the age of eighty, Izzy published *The Trial of Socrates*, which was a national bestseller. He wrote the book after he taught himself ancient Greek.

BENJAMIN C. BRADLEE was for nearly thirty years the charismatic editorial leader of *The Washington Post*. It was Ben who gave the *Post* the range and courage to pursue such historic issues as Watergate. He supported his reporters with a tenacity that made them fearless and it is no accident that so many became authors of influential, best-selling books.

ROBERT L. BERNSTEIN, the chief executive of Random House for more than a quarter century, guided one of the nation's premier publishing houses. Bob was personally responsible for many books of political dissent and argument that challenged tyranny around the globe. He is also the founder and longtime chair of Human Rights Watch, one of the most respected human rights organizations in the world.

• • •

For fifty years, the banner of Public Affairs Press was carried by its owner Morris B. Schnapper, who published Gandhi, Nasser, Toynbee, Truman, and about 1,500 other authors. In 1983, Schnapper was described by *The Washington Post* as "a redoubtable gadfly." His legacy will endure in the books to come.

Peter Osnos, *Founder*